Building a Web Site

on the internet

A practical guide to writing and commissioning web pages

Brendan Murphy

www.internet-handbooks.co.uk

Other Internet Handbooks by the same author

Finding a Job on the Internet

First published in 2000 by Internet Handbooks, a Division of International Briefings Ltd, Plymbridge House, Estover Road, Plymouth PL6 7PY, United Kingdom.

Customer services tel:	(01752) 202301
Orders fax:	(01752) 202333
Customer services email:	cservs@plymbridge.com
Distributors web site:	http://www.plymbridge.com
Internet Handbooks web site:	http://www.internet-handbooks.co.uk

Note: The contents of this book are offered for the purposes of general guidance only and no liability can be accepted for any loss or expense incurred as a result of relying in particular circumstances on statements made in this book. Readers are advised to check the current position with the appropriate authorities before entering into personal arrangements.

Case studies in this book are entirely fictional and any resemblance to real persons or organisations is entirely coincidental.

Printed and bound by The Cromwell Press Ltd, Trowbridge, Wiltshire.

Contents

Contents ....

Contents

Contents ....

List of illustrations

Illustrations...

Preface

It's about four years since I began to think about the internet. In my first couple of months of surfing I felt that, although it was fun, it didn't really serve any particular purpose. I've come a good way since those days and now conduct a substantial amount of personal, educational and business communication over the internet. Indeed, the internet has revolutionised my entire working and private life. From my professional work, to ordering books and CDs, browsing home shopping pages, having computer programming queries answered from a Canadian helpline, through to communicating weekly with a friend in Australia – and even listening to live radio broadcasts from around the world – the internet has become a truly indispensable tool in my life.

The past two years have seen a huge increase in the number of companies offering cheap access to the internet. Email, web space and other services are all being offered free of charge. Indeed, the only payment required nowadays is often the local rate telephone call used to access the internet – and in some cases that too is free! High street stores, banks and even supermarkets now offer a very inexpensive route to access this extraordinary communications and entertainment tool.

A recent massive growth area of the internet has been the number of organisations and individuals developing web pages. These offer an online 24-hours-a-day worldwide presence. It is here that I hope the book will help you. By the time you have finished I hope you'll have all the skills needed to join in the online revolution. You will be able to build great web pages that will both attract and keep visitors from all over the world. The book is organised to help you get the maximum value in the shortest space of time.

I'd like to clear up a point of constant confusion for internet users. With the increased use of the internet for personal, educational and business purposes, the terms and the technologies are becoming overlapping and mixed up. For all practical purposes, terms such as the 'internet', 'net', 'world wide web' and 'web' can be considered synonymous.

▶ Part One of the book gives a brief history of the internet, and advice on how to get started with a computer, modem and internet service provider (ISP). There is also a word about browsers and the best way to search the web. Some thoughts on the future direction of the web are offered, to help you keep your thinking ahead of work colleagues and neighbours.

▶ Part Two challenges you to get down to the serious business of building a great web site. Spanner in hand, you'll learn, in a straightforward way, all the basic tools and tricks required to master hyper text markup language (HTML), the wordprocessing-type language used to create web pages. You will be surprised at how easy it is.

▶ For those of you looking to build web pages without getting involved with HTML, Part Three introduces six different tools that will easily do the job for you. By the end you'll have everything you need to make good progress with your web site.

▶ Part Four offers advice for people thinking of using the services of a third party supplier. Disappointment and frustration can often arise when other people become involved. This part of the book will help you manage your web projects effectively. It will also show you how to get the best value for money from your investment. The book finishes with a selection of useful web sites and organisations to help you get the most from your web design plans.

As a professional web user – and an author who loves to hear the views of his readers – I hope you'll begin communicating with me online. Those who use this service will join an élite group of readers who are sharing information about interesting internet materials which we encounter on the net.

Meantime I hope that you have fun with this book, and wish you the very best in developing your own successful web site. Good luck!

Brendan Murphy
brendanmurphy@internet-handbooks.co.uk

1 Internet basics

In this chapter we will explore:

▶ *the importance of the internet*
▶ *a brief history of the internet and the world wide web*
▶ *choosing hardware and software to get you online*
▶ *choosing an internet service provider (ISP)*
▶ *choosing the best browser*
▶ *searching for information on the internet*
▶ *questions and answers*
▶ *case studies*

. . . .

Understanding the importance of the internet

The rise in usage of the internet over the last five years has been explosive. Whilst it is very difficult to quote definitive statistics, recent figures suggest that there will be an estimated 250 million users world-wide by 2004. For hobbyists and educationalists, through to business users, the internet is fast becoming the preferred form of modern day communication. Access is global, inexpensive, visual, and instant. All you need is a standard PC, a modem and a telephone line, and away you go. The neat thing about the internet is that everyone can have their say. You don't have to be a big business, or a large college or university. A private individual can potentially have the same presence as big corporations – and it's all done from your home PC.

Using the internet for a purpose
If you've ever used the internet, you can't help but notice how many business transactions are now being carried out on it. From home shopping to flight reservations, from the transfer of huge business-to-business funds to the downloading of music onto personal stereos, and the playing of live radio and TV online, the rise has been dramatic.

With the rise in the availability of free space on the web, the development of home pages by organisations and individuals has rocketed.

▶ *Home page* – The first page that users see when they visit your web site. This page usually holds all the links to other internal and external pages and generally acts as an overall index to your web site. Whether you're trying to sell something, buy something or just publish some detail of your personal life, the web page is a great tool to use. More and more organisations and individuals are using their internet presence to open up whole new avenues to explore in their business and private lives.

Internet basics...

Fig. 1. A simple representation of the internet – a vast network of computers circling the globe.

A brief history of the internet and the world wide web

The internet is a worldwide network of computers connected in a common manner allowing ease of access both for communicating and for transferring data. The internet covers the four corners of the world and so can be considered to be truly global. Conjuring up visions of fast cars heading off down the freeway, the internet is also known as the 'information superhighway' and you'll soon see why this name fits pretty much perfectly.

But how did it all begin? Back in 1969, at the height of the Cold War, the American Department of Defense devised a system for maintaining communication through the telephone network across the USA in the event of a nuclear attack disrupting the telephone system. This system, ARPANet (Advanced Research Projects Agency Network), is generally considered to have been the birth of the internet, and took around ten years to develop.

An alternative, but equally credible view, is that the internet was created to enable academic research funds in 1960s America to be better used; universities needed a robust method of easily transfering and sharing information. Although today's internet is highly sophisti-cated, this first usage saw messages between two computers find their way through the telephone lines, trying different routes should some not be available, until they reached their destination. The founda-tions of this system saw the development of the standard TCP/IP – transport control protocol/internet protocol – still used today to allow us access to the network.

Further development soon followed. By the mid 1970s the internet was becoming big in universities and research institutions, offering a great means of sharing research information amongst academics. Things sailed along pretty much happily over the coming years until around 1980, when control of this network was taken over by the Internet Architecture Board (IAB). In 1989, the internet was to change forever when, in the CERN laboratories in Switzerland, a group of researchers came up with the World Wide Web (WWW). Today control of the internet rests with a number of organisations having some impressive-sounding names. To the average internet user, however, it belongs to ordinary people. We can all use it to communicate effectively, we can publish on it, and we can transact a fair amount of daily business on it. If you are connected, you are as much in control of 'the internet' as anybody else!

Understanding the world wide web (WWW)
The world wide web – WWW, or web, for short – was developed to allow physicists anywhere to communicate easily on the internet using simple hypertext access to information sources. Over the following years, this concept evolved, to the dismay of some stuffy academics, to include documents that incorporated sound and even video. Hyper-text documents allow users to click on 'hot spots', commonly a word or picture, which then allows them to access further detail represented by the word or picture. This can be thought of as 'drill down' where, by

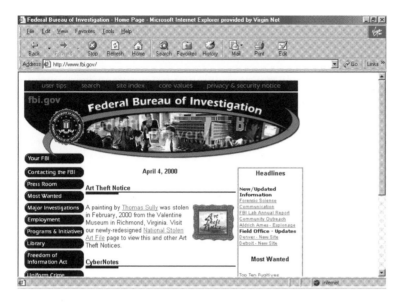

Fig. 2. The home page of the US Federal Bureau of Investigation (FBI), one of the most visited pages on the internet.

simple mouse-clicking, a subject is expanded and extended, on each click. Where this method of access leads to different documents then it's known as 'hyperlinks'. The web page in Figure 2, for example, shows the home page details for the Federal Bureau of Investigation (FBI).

Choosing hardware and software to get you online

When looking at hardware and software specifications, buy as big as you can afford! This may not be the most sophisticated technical advice, but in practical terms it's pretty accurate and good advice to follow when choosing a suitable PC and modem. The following table offers some information on the typical sizes you should be looking at when purchasing hardware:

PC component	Requirement	Comments
Central processing unit (CPU)	Pentium III, 450 megahertz	A really fast chip that will run your applications very quickly.
Random access memory (RAM)	32MB minimum, 64MB preferred, 128MB if possible	Will allow large programs to load more quickly.
Monitor	15' or 17'	Buy what you can afford.
Hard disk	6.4 gigabytes (GB) or more	The more hard disk space you have, the more programs and data you can store.
CD drive	48-speed upwards	Determines how fast programs will run from compact discs.
Backup unit	See your dealer	A must! Don't risk losing your valuable data.
Modem	56K internal/external	The faster the modem, the faster web pages will load from the internet to your PC.

Fig. 3. The Virgin Net logon screen. The person's user name is based on their email address. By checking the 'remember password' box, your password will be inserted automatically each time you log on.

Choosing an internet service provider (ISP)

An internet service provider (ISP) is any a commercial organisation that sells access to the internet. It's just like choosing a telephone provider on the basis of the best service to meet your particular audio needs. Choose your ISP in the same way. When you buy into an ISP, you normally get some software, and a user identification and password that allows you to sign-up and access the internet.

ISPs generally fit into two main types: those that charge for their services and those that don't. For those ISPs who charge for their service, it is common for them to provide a 'try before you buy' option. This will normally give you a limited period – usually a calendar month, or 50 or 100 free hour – so that you can try out their services. A word of caution: to get your free trial you'll have to give your credit or debit card details. After the free period has expired, you will continue to be charged unless you specifically cancel the agreement. It's also worth pointing out that the type of advert that goes something like 'Join now, 100 free hours online!' can often be misleading. The allocation of free hours must usually be used in the first month of registration with the ISP – great if you don't mind staying up all night and running up large phone bills!

Free ISPs don't levy monthly subscription charges for using their service but rather rely on advertising and expensive telephone support charges (50p to £1 a minute) to provide a source of revenue. These ISPs also cream off a small percentage of the cost of the call made to your phone company when you use their service. Both types of ISP normally

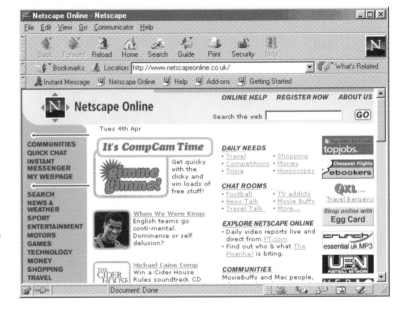

Fig. 4. The home page of Netscape Online. As well as distributing its popular browser (Netsacpe Navigator), Netscape also offers a host of online services ranging from software downloads to news and shopping.

offer between three and ten separate email addresses, and various 'unique' services on their own private network. These could include weather reports, search facilities, news updates and specialist interest areas for children and adults. Indeed, some ISPs offer so many private services that you can often meet all your day-to-day needs by simply surfing in these areas!

With ISPs who charge a monthly subscription you will also have a number of free hours to surf, extra hours being charged at an agreed rate. More recently, ISPs have begun to offer completely free access to the internet and this typically might allow you three hours free access a month. That's completely free – you don't even pay for the telephone call.

Free web space

All ISPs offer some free web space with their internet access packages. This can vary from as little as 5 megabytes to an average of 10 to 20 megabytes, or even unlimited space offered by a few ISPs. So, how do you decide how much web space you'll need? This should help you decide:

► *1 megabyte (or MB)* = 1 million characters where a character is any letter, number or punctuation mark. This book is around 45,000 words long, and the average word length is seven letters (including one space between each word). If the book were to be loaded into some free web space it would occupy around one third of a megabyte. This calculation is rough and ready, and doesn't take into account the use of graphics which are very large. Still, as you can see, 10MB is an awful lot of free space and could probably hold the contents of around 30 similar books!

Most ISPs offer software tools to help you build web pages easily, and we'll talk about these in Part Three.

Call charges

Telephone call charges are well worth a separate mention. Even if you are only paying local rates, surfing the web can sometimes prove expensive. Make sure that your ISP dial-up number is included in any discount package (such as BT's Friends and Family) offered by your phone company. This will help you keep costs to an acceptable level.

Checklist for choosing an ISP

1. Find out whether you have to pay any costs to use the service, over and above your telephone call charges.
2. Make sure that access is charged at local – not national – call rates.
3. Find out how much free web space is provided (so you can publish your web pages).
4. Ensure that an adequate number of email addresses are included.
5. Make sure that a fast access speed is available for your modem.
6. Ensure that adequate support is provided (especially telephone support) and that these calls are charged at an acceptable call rate per minute.

7. Find out what value added services are provided.
8. Find out if there are any free monthly hours available (no call charges).
9. Make sure that your private address details will not be passed on to any other online organisation or other third party (this will stop the electronic equivalent of junk mail 'spam' – appearing in your email system).
10. The following table shows the home page addresses for a selection of the major ISPs available in the United Kingdom:

Name	Monthly charge?*	Web site address	Email addresses	Web space
America Online	yes	www.aol.co.uk	5	10mb
BT Internet	yes	www.btinternet.com	5	10mb
Compuserve	yes	www.compuserve.co.uk	1	5mb
CurrantBun	free	www.currantbun.com	unlimited	5mb
Freeserve	free	www.freeserve.net	unlimited	15mb
Netscape Online	free	www.netscapeonline.co.uk	unlimited	20mb
TescoNet	free	www.tesco.net	5	10mb
UUNet	yes	www.dial.pipex.com	5	15mb
Virgin Net	free	www.virgin.net	5	10mb
WHSmith	free	www.whsmith.co.uk	unlimited	unlimited

*correct at time of publication

Using cybercafes

As well as having your own ISP, you can also access the internet by visiting a cybercafe or internet cafe. As the names suggest, these are cafes that offer internet access along with a cup of coffee and a bun! Many bookstores also offer internet access, and again this may be an option for those who do not have access to a personal computer. In fact, using the internet in a specialist centre is often very relaxing and sociable, turning on its head the often quoted anti-social nature of internet use. Some smaller locally-based companies also act as ISPs, however they don't generally offer any value added services. These centres, however, can sometimes offer faster internet access speeds, since they have fewer users.

▶ *Caution* – If you use a small company, and it goes bust, you could find yourself not only having to hook up with a new ISP but also having to change your email address, confusing friends and organisations who may have stored your details in their internet address book files.

Choosing the best browser

What is a browser? Think of it as a mini telephone system. You've got your phone (your PC), you know the number of the person or organisa-

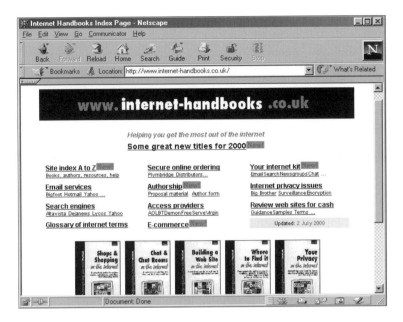

Fig. 5. What the Netscape Navigator 4.0 browser looks like. The toolbars across the top give you access to email, a personal address book, search, bookmarks, history list, Page Composer, newsgroups, and many other handy features.

tion you want to talk to (their web site address or email address), and you just need something to dial them up (the browser). Connect the three together, and you have instant access to a world of information.

Figures 5 and 6 illustrate the entry screens you will find with Netscape Navigator and Microsoft Internet Explorer, by far the two most widely used web browsers.

Getting a free browser from your ISP

Don't worry about buying browser software, since the ISP you join up with will provide all the browser software you need internet. The only time that you might choose browser software is if you had some particular reason for favouring a particular product. Microsoft has the lion's share of the market, mainly as a result of their commercial success in getting it preloaded onto so many new PCs.

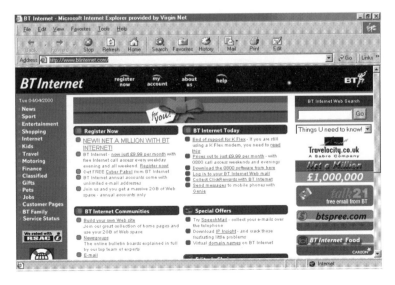

Fig. 6. What the Internet Explorer browser looks like. The toolbars across the top give you access to Outlook Express (for email, a personal address book, and newsgroups) plus 'favourites' (your bookmarked web sites), a history list, search, and many other handy features.

19

You should upgrade your browser from time to time, to the latest version available. The particular browser's home page on the web is the place to go, but beware – these browsers could take an hour or so to download. Fortunately, most of the reputable monthly internet/PC magazines carry new and free versions of browsers on the CDs supplied with each edition.

Searching for information on the internet

The web has over a billion pages of useful information (and some not so useful). This figure is growing at a fantastic rate. Each page has its own specific address, called a URL (uniform resource locator). To remember the URLs of all the pages you want to access would be akin to memorising a telephone directory – impossible. Never fear, all those geeks at the software companies that write programs for the web have provided an array of tools ('search engines') that let you look, very easily, for just about anything.

All the search engines operate in a similar way. You type in a keyword, for example 'cars'. Within a few seconds, the search engine displays on your screen all the associated pages containing the keyword in their description. Be careful if you type in just one common word like 'cars', it could compile you a list of over a million web pages! Let's now introduce some of the common search engines.

AltaVista
http://www.altavista.com/
AltaVista, from the Digital corporation, will probably return the most pages from the keyword(s) that you enter. The main screen, shown below, allows you to enter the term that you wish to search on, choose whether to search on the complete web or only certain sites, and choose the language to be searched on (so choosing 'English' will

Fig. 7. The home page of AltaVista, one of the half dozen most popular search engines on the internet, used by millions of people every day. The search service is completely free. The search box (Find this:') is in the middle of the screen. Type in anything you want to find out about, and click Search.

return only those web pages composed in English – great for filtering out unnecessary pages).

Yahoo!
http://www.yahoo.com/
The ever popular Yahoo! database has four main categories which it searches through on entry of a keyword. Documents are then displayed in order of relevance. Yahoo! also has a 'yellow pages' option that allows you to easily locate business user home pages.

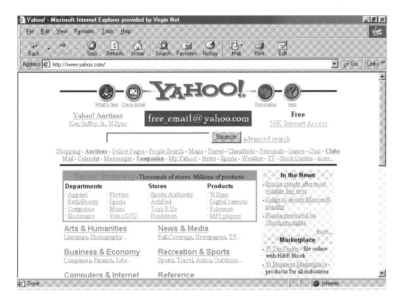

Fig. 8. The home page of Yahoo!, perhaps the biggest and most popular of all the search facilities on the internet. It is really a gigantic structured information directory. You can 'drill down' its many category headings, until you find what you want.

Fig. 9. The home page of Lycos, another of the half dozen top search engines on the internet. You can either use type your query into the search box in the middle of the screen, or click on any of the underlined headings (hyperlinks) to find the information you want.

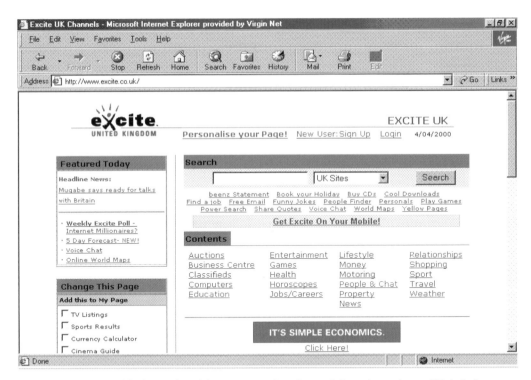

Fig. 10. The home page of Excite, another of the top ten search engines and directories on the net. This is the home page of its UK section. Like all the main search engines, its search facility is completely free.

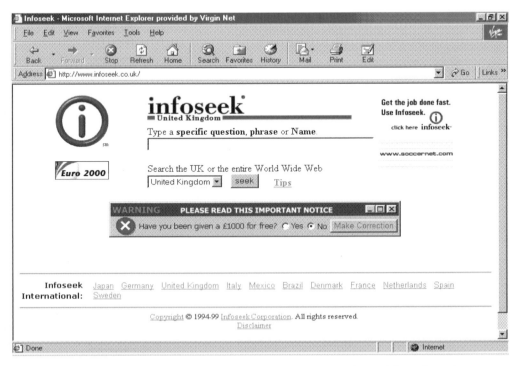

Fig. 11. The Infoseek home page. Infoseek is another of the top ten free search engines and directories on the net. This is its UK home page, as you can tell from the web address in the location panel in the upper part of the illustration.

22

Fig. 12. The Webcrawler home page – an alternative to Infoseek, Yahoo! and the other free search services on the internet.

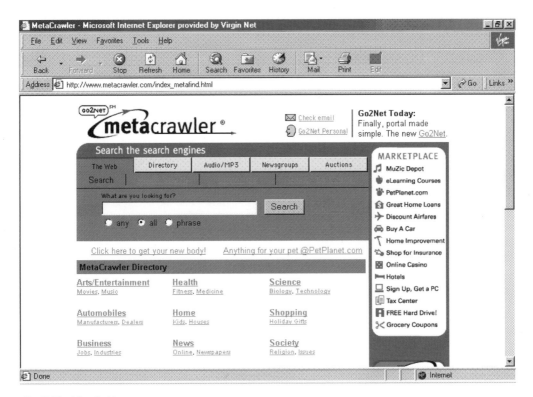

Fig. 13. The Metafind home page.

Lycos
http://www.lycos.com/
Lycos operates similarly to Yahoo! with the entry of a keyword, then the choice of where to look for it. Lycos is particularly easy to use. It has a useful utility that lets you click on whether you want to find documents containing all of your keywords or documents that contain any of your keywords.

Excite
http://www.excite.co.uk/
Excite does all the same things as the other search engines. You type in a keyword, choose where to search, click, and wait a few seconds for the results to be displayed. However, Excite goes a little bit further: it also looks for pages that are closely linked to the keywords that you enter. For example, should you enter the keywords 'Scottish Lochs', Excite recognises the link between Scottish and Scotland and will provide details of pages associated with Scotland as well as the requested pages associated with 'Scottish Lochs.'

Infoseek
http://www.infoseek.co.uk/
Using Infoseek is a piece of cake. By simply entering suitable key-word(s) Infoseek trundles off and returns the pages that you are looking for, simple! Infoseek also designates over 500,000 web sites as 'Infoseek Select Sites', as being in their eyes particularly interesting.

Webcrawler
http://www.webcrawler.com/
Webcrawler uses 'natural language searching'. This allows you to key in just what you are looking for, without having to learn any of the more little tricks required to search any more than one word in other search engines.

Give it a try!
The above explanation can only really touch the surface of using a search engine. The only way to really understand what each can do for you is to jump in to their home pages and have a look. You will soon find out which one(s) you prefer to use.

Using metasearchers for comprehensive searching
The search engines listed above, and many others, operate independently from each other. That means that the results may vary from one search engine to another. A metasearcher allows you to enter a term to be searched and have the metasearcher carry out the search for you over multiple search engines. This ensures that you get the most thorough search of the web available. Metasearchers can be more difficult to use than straightforward search engines, but the results are impressive – especially if you are searching for an obscure subject. The following metasearchers are worth a look:

MetaBug	www.metabug.com
MetaFind	www.metafind.com
Go2Net	www.go2net.com
SuperCrawler	www.supercrawler.com

Questions and answers

Which ISP is best?

Your choice of ISP will largely depend on the requirements you have for using the web. Some ISPs are heavily subscribed and can often appear slow to use, whilst others offer faster connections. If your internet needs are purely personal, then any of the free ISPs will provide you with all you need to effectively use the web. If you're a business user, you might be better off paying a small monthly charge to ensure that all the value-added services, such as inexpensive phone support and fast connections, are provided.

Which browser should I choose, Netscape Navigator or Internet Explorer?

Netscape has been around the longest and cornered the browser market early on. Microsoft however, has since been very successful, largely through shipping a copy of Internet Explorer with every copy of its Windows 95, Windows 98, Office 97 and Office 2000 products. More recently, both browsers have become free with bundled CDs attached to computing magazines, so it's now quite easy to install both and decide which one you prefer yourself.

What is a metasearcher?

A metasearcher is software that searches through the common search engines available on the web to provide you with a comprehensive search of your query. The results returned are split into the best match to your query, split by each of the common search engines.

Case studies

Phil installs a free ISP

Phil has recently bought a home PC which came with a CD for Virgin Net. After nervously following the online step-by-step instructions, Phil was happily surprised to find that he was surfing the web, and had sent his first email, within an hour of installing the software. The following day he realised with a shock that he had spent six continuous hours online.

Louise takes up picture-framing

Louise has recently taken up picture framing as a hobby. After searching the web using Webcrawler, she has found, and contacted, ten indivi-duals interested in her particular specialisation of creating frames using reclaimed driftwood. Could she have used another online route to provide a comprehensive search of the web?

2 The future of the web

In this chapter we will explore:

► *online shopping*

► *ecommerce: buying and selling on the web*

► *keeping transactions secure online*

► *the future for businesses and individuals*

► *questions and answers*

► *case studies*

. . . .

Online shopping

Visiting online shops: some great sites to visit

The web really is a shoppers' paradise. It doesn't matter what you want to buy or sell, there's sure to be someone who'll want to do business with you. In the past two years, the rise in online shopping sites has been tremendous, with thousands of companies offering new online services almost daily. Provided the web site you visit uses one of the security measures outlined below (or some other method that you feel comfortable with) then shopping online can be a great experience, offering great choice and great value for money. The following sites are worth a visit.

Amazon Bookstore
http://www.amazon.co.uk
Amazon really shows you how to successfully transact business on the web. This hugely popular site is jam-packed with over 1.5 million book titles, CDs and other items to tempt the cyber-visitor. Once you purchase

Fig. 14. The home page of Amazon, famous as the biggest shop on the internet. It is best known as an online bookshop, but has expanded rapidly into other areas such as music, DVD and video, and even auctions and other services. It has recently merged with the media giant Time-Warner.

a book from Amazon you can even write an online review allowing others to make a decision before buying. The author of a book can also leave some narrative about his or her masterpiece (visit Amazon and see what this author, Brendan Murphy, has said about this book, *Building a Web Site on the Internet*!).

You also have the opportunity to find details very easily of an author's complete works as well as look at other books that people buying the same items as you bought. Amazon also offers gift certificates as well as a number of charts detailing top selling items in various book and CD categories. Amazon also invites you to join their organisation as an associate, and here, by providing links from your web site, you can make money on books bought by your visitors – ecommerce at work!

QXL auctions
http://www.qxl.com

Remember that first holiday on the Mediterranean? Or the first visit to the local market? If you weren't happy with the price of an item you walked away, only to be recalled by the stall or shop owner to 'discuss and agree' a suitable price – great fun. With QXL the same concept applies (without

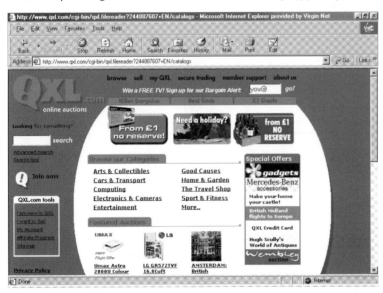

Fig. 15. The home page of QXL auctions. QXL stands for 'quick sell'. QXL has established itself as the UK and European market leader in online auctions, and competes with the hugely popular American online auctioneer, eBay

the glorious Mediterranean sunshine!). Here you can browse through articles from everyday people, collectors, retailers and even QXL them-selves. QXL auctions allow you to check current bids, up them, and even place a maximum price which will be managed by a robot who will bid on your behalf. If you're outbid for an item an email will be sent telling you this giving you the chance to place a higher bid. When the auction is closed you'll be informed if you've won and be given information on how to go about paying and receiving your purchase.

UK High Street Fashion Stores
http://www.principles.co.uk

Visit this web page and gain access to a number of branded High Street fashion chains. Choose from Burton's, Dorothy Perkins, Evans, Hawkshead, Principles for Men and many more stores and buy the latest fashions online. Each page offers a number of great competitions as well as many special offers.

Interflora
http://www.interflora.co.uk
Can't find time to send that much awaited bouquet of flowers for an anniversary or special occasion? The Interflora site provides a great method of choosing and sending flowers throughout the UK and throughout the world. This site also offers a handy organiser that will remind you by email of any important anniversaries or occasions throughout the year that might require flowers to be sent. There is also a gift search utility that lets you quickly select an appropriate gift for that 'hard-to-buy-for' relative or friend.

Fig. 16. The home page of Interflora, showing a professional approach to online retailing. All the images in the browser window are hyperlinks. By clicking on one you will be taken to a different area of the web site.

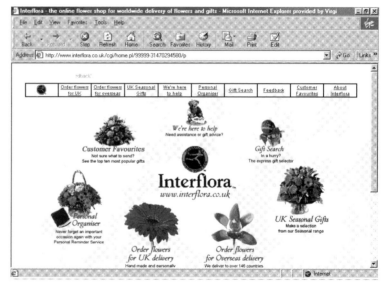

Chateau Wines online
http://www.chateauonline.com
This web site really does provide a very comprehensive source of information on wines and their appropriate uses. It offers advice on choosing wines for certain occasions, moods and foods, as well as offering great bargains on bulk purchases. Like all good wine merchants, Chateau have on hand their very own Sommelier who will help guide you through the assault course to finding that perfect tipple.

Direct Lenses
http://www.directlenses.com
Run by registered opticians, Direct Lenses offers a cheap and easy way to purchase disposable contact lenses. Passing on volume of scale and the benefit of reduced overheads, buying lenses online could be the new easy way to buy for busy people. Direct Lenses require in the first instance to contact your optitian to obtain a copy of your prescription

and to ensure that you've had a contact lens consultation within the last 12 months.

Funstore
http://www.funstore.co.uk
This is a great little web site that takes you into a toy and game store that is made up of many floors. Simply click the 'lift' button and ride the elevator to the department of your choice. Alternatively, grab hold of your personal shopper and let him help you find the perfect gift. Funstore guarantees first class post delivery in around 48 hours from your order being placed.

Fig. 17. The home page of Funstore, an online toys and games store for the UK. In some ways resembles that of Interflora (figure 16): its illustrated hyperlinks help you start exploring its web site.

Ecommerce: buying and selling on the web

The popular term used to describe trading over the internet either as a buyer or as a seller, is electronic commerce – ecommerce for short. Ecommerce sites allow for the safe transaction of money either through a secure connection or through the use of digital cash. The rise in companies offering goods and services for sale over the web has been dramatic. The benefits of doing business online are many:

1. reduced floor space required
2. reduced overheads
3. opens up your business to a global marketplace
4. increased sales potential

At the moment the main items for sale on the web are smaller items such as books, CDs, flowers and clothing. However the challenge over the coming years will be to transform the way that consumers buy large items such as cars and even houses.

This is a great time to look at developing a web site that offers goods and services for sale. The following checklist should provide some food for thought should you be considering setting up an online sales outlet:

Your checklist for selling on the web

1. Provide a comprehensive service to your customers. This should include contact details, product guides, specifications, information sheets, phone directories, a searchable database and great images of your products and services.

2. Offer incentives to your customers to use your online service (offer an online discount).

3. Create a mailing list and keep your customers informed.

4. Keep an online profile of what each customer buys – use this for targeted marketing.

5. Include links to web sites that compliment your product or service. Negotiate a deal with these other companies to receive payment should one of your customers buy their product.

6. Make your site interesting and include something that will make people return regularly (monthly competitions, free gifts etc.).

7. Avoid making your site hard to understand – it's easy for customers to surf elsewhere.

Keeping transactions secure online

The main issue that concerns both buyers and sellers on the web, is security. It is unlikely that a business will be successful in developing an online service if consumers feel vulnerable about sending debit or credit card details over the web. At the present time, there are a couple of security standards (or protocols to use the technical word) that help ensure online security.

Secure sockets layer (SSL)
SSL was developed by Netscape and allows the transfer of private documents across the internet. You'll know that the web site you're on is using SSL if the address (or URL) of the page you're on starts with the 'https://'. SSL is the most common system used for credit and debit transactions and all the major retailers use it. Look out for the little padlock or key at the bottom of your screen. Its appearance means that you are making a secure connection.

Secure electronic transaction (SET)
SET is the new kid on the block. It is supported by the big boys such as Visa and Mastercard. The system operates by utilising 'digital signatures.' A digital signature is a code that is unique to an individual and is attached to any digital transaction that an individual conducts over the web. The digital signature can only be associated with one single person and so acts as proof of identity (just like the signature on the back of your credit card!). Digital signatures are unforgeable and this is achieved by encrypting them. The benefit of this system is that the seller does not see your

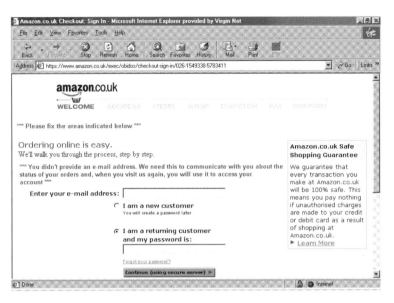

Fig. 18. The Amazon safe ordering screen. The web address no longer begins with 'http' but https'. The letter 's' signifies that it is a secure page. All communications from this page between you and the company will be fully encrypted and thus protected from hackers and eavesdroppers.

credit card number but rather it is transferred to your credit card company for automated billing thus lessening the risk of any security breach of your personal information.

Digital cash
Another of the many ways to conduct business over the web is by using 'digital cash.' Digital cash is very like real cash in that it is completely anonymous. At the moment you have absolutely no idea who has had bank notes in your pocket before you, or what they have been used for. Digital cash works on the same principle. Banks issue digital cash certificates which you can use over the web to buy goods – these certificates will be worth monetary values such as £5, £10 and so on. When companies receive these certificates they cash them in through any bank and the digital cash is again available for re-use just like real cash. The great advantage of the system over others is the anonymity factor. Using digital cash will ensure that your debit/credit card details do not become available for misuse by hackers or others online.

Setting the standard
It is worth mentioning that the methods used to pay for online transactions at present are many. Hopefully, over the coming years, an adopted standard will evolve which will ensure maximum security, flexibility and privacy for online shoppers.

The future for businesses and individuals

The internet in its most popular sense is still a relatively new technology. It is still developing and growing at a rate that can be hard to keep pace with. New ideas or ways of doing things are devised almost daily. Many companies are offering new products desperate to be the one that establishes the standard in a key area. The following list of technologies just scratches the surface of what may appear over the next five to ten years. It is a taster of things to come.

Intranets

Simply explained, an intranet is an internal internet. It looks and feels the same as the big internet. The main difference is that it is private and normally available only to staff, associates and possibly customers and suppliers of one organisation. An intranet uses the same HTML pages to display information, uses the same browsers to view that information and is underpinned by the same protocol (TCP/IP.)

Intranets offer companies a great way to keep employees informed. News items, telephone directories, product catalogues and many other items of useful information can be made available round the clock for staff. Intranets increase communication, and allow updates and changes to company documentation to be done quickly. In this way, employees have the most up-to-date picture all of the time. Some company intranets now include audio and even video, providing a more personable way to pass on an important message or deliver training. Intranets are becoming ever more popular amongst large organisations. This popularity is sure to filter down into smaller organisations in the coming years.

Conferencing

In a bid to reduce accommodation and travel costs, as well as to increase productivity, companies have found the internet a great medium for business conferencing. The following types of conferences are likely to gain in popularity and usage in the coming years.

▶ *Bulletin board conferences* - A conference is set up by a moderator, who gives access to the conference area to authorised individuals. This conference area appears on your desktop once you log in to the conference software system. Members of the conference then have access to read and write messages to the conference. These mes-

Fig. 19. The Open University desktop area for students and teachers. The icons dotted about the page give online access to everything from tutors' areas to reference databases and online conferences.

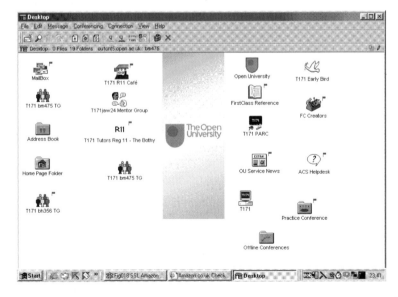

sages can be sent to a particular member, or to the whole conference, allowing it to be read by others. The conference may be set up for a few hours, days or weeks depending on the subject under discussion. Real-time discussion is usually also available so that when you're online leaving a comment, you might be invited to discuss it further in real-time mode. The Open University – Britain's largest higher education institution and a leader in using the web as a vehicle for teaching – increasingly uses this method for online student tutorial topics as well as for lecturer support.

▶ *Real-time conferencing* – Real-time conferencing refers to online conversations between two or more users. It allows questions and answers to be typed at a keyboard and the information made instantaneously available for others to comment or reply. For example, if you type a question someone will almost immediately type a live answer, which you can see appearing on your screen in a few seconds. This type of conference is often referred to as chat, or IRC ('internet relay chat'). It can be carried out using software such as 'Cu-See-Me' and Microsoft's 'NetMeeting' as well as by using ICQ ('I Seek You') software.

▶ *Audio conferencing* - Given the costs of long distance telephone calls, audio conferencing is becoming ever more popular. By having a specialised piece of software and a microphone at both ends, you can now easily talk with people from all around the world in real time. At the moment the quality of the sound is imperfect, but this is sure to improve over coming years.

Bandwidth

All of the above types of internet conferencing will become ever more popular only if bandwidths increase. The bandwidth of a connection determines the both the speed and amount of data that can be carried over that connection. Video and audio files are very large. If the bandwidth is small, such files can become distorted and appear to be out of time. Increased bandwidths using fast connections such as ISDN lines and cable networks will increase the quality of images and sounds. This will make conferencing over the internet more attractive as a communication medium.

Internet2

In the old stuffy days of the internet (the late 1960s and early 1970s), the academics who controlled the system frowned if it was used for anything remotely commercial or trivial. The evolution of today's internet has of course seen this medium turn into an entertainment channel to surpass all others (as well as still maintaining a great base for academics!) and this has incensed more than a few people. To counter the current internet revolution, a consortium of US universities with links to European institutions has developed Internet2. Internet2 is a high bandwith network that is open only to invited users. This ensures that speed and exclusivity are maintained. The development of Internet2 could be seen as a competitor for the internet as we currently know it.

The future of the web

Wireless application protocol (WAP)
You can't help noticing the proliferation of palmtops and those ubiquitous mobile phones. Needless to say, the internet has also reached this type of appliance. WAP is designed to facilitate web access to palmtops and mobile phones and other hand-held devices. This new protocol also offers a special form of HTML, known as wireless markup language (WML). This language can be used to deliver the look and functionality of the web to portable communications devices.

The future for individuals

Online shops
The success of online shopping for business transactions has spawned an industry that makes it easy for you to join the ranks of the ecommerce magnates. By adding some links to your web site you can have all the security and functionality of the big companies at a fraction of the cost. Setting up an online shop is now very easy to do and allows safe transactions to be made across the Internet. Yahoo!, the world's most popular search engine, offers this service through its 'online stores.' This allows you to set up shop for a monthly fee of around $100, for which Yahoo! guarantees safe credit card transactions between you and your customers as well as the management of your online services. Compare this with the cost of setting up a shop in a real high street, with the landlord's rent and escalating business rates demanded by the local council! Online it's easy, profitable and fun!

Fig. 20. Yahoo!Store. Yahoo! has developed a system whereby anyone can set up a Yahoo! store. There is a template-based design. You can add products into a catalogue and display them on the screen. Your customers can even pay by credit card online. Thousands of enterprises small and large have taken advantage of this service.

Mondex Card
A Mondex card is one with a computer chip embedded in it. It can then act as an electronic purse which can be shared between many accounts such as video club membership, library membership, and store cards. The Mondex card contains money added from an autoteller and that money can then be spent electronically from the purse. This type of smartcard

34

could eventually replace multiple cards for credit, debit, and member-ships.

WebTV

WebTV offers users the familiarity of the television set with the benefits of surfing the web and using email. Microsoft bought WebTV in 1996 and since this time has installed a number of pilots around the USA. With WebTV your normal TV set has a decoder on top, allowing a modem to deliver web services. The traditional aerial continues to provide your TV services. This type of product offers great benefits to the elderly, for example, who might not be comfortable with a PC but are happy to experiment with their TV set. WebTV allows interaction to take place with TV programs via icons and text overlays that provide further informa-tion concerning the program being viewed. Many cable and digital TV companies offer similar or complementary services to WebTV.

Video streaming

A great development over the web has been the arrival of streamed video files. Video files are laborious to download from the web, because of their size, and the limited bandwidth. This means that to play a video clip, you first have to download the whole thing and then play it through a piece of software resident on your PC. With video streaming, 'real-time' video is available. Using a buffering technique, special 'streaming' software starts playing the video file even while it is downloading onto your PC. This allows great quality sound and pictures to be transmitted from anywhere in the world in virtually real time.

Fig. 21. The home page of Realplayer, producers of software that helps you download and listen to music over the internet.

The future of the web ....

Downloading music from the web

One of the fastest growing uses of internet technology is the downloading of digital music files. This phenomenon has grown due to the invention of Media Player 3 (MP3) format. This hugely popular file format allows audio files to be compressed to around 5% of their original size whilst still retaining excellent sound quality. Tiny hand-held MP3 personal players are now available in the high street and many music artists have made MP3 files available for download to these personal players. In the near future, you will be able to pay for and download your favourite group's new album, or mix and match to create a 'best of' album for yourself.

Questions and answers

Is it safe to give credit card details over the web?

As long as the company you are dealing with is reputable and offers a secure connection, it is quite safe to use your credit card. Always look out for the yellow or gold padlock or key symbol; this lights up at the bottom of your browser screen when you enter a secure site. You can also tell that a site is secure if its web address starts with https, rather than just http. Or look for some other guarantee before giving over personal details. Steer clear of sites that require you to send your credit card details via an email message.

How can I keep up to date on new internet-based technologies?

Your ISP should be your first port of call for information. Most ISP home pages are full of news items about the latest internet advances. Also, for as little as £1.99 per month you can buy a subscription to an easy-to-read, information-packed internet magazine; the titles are plentiful and are a great source of up-to-date, expert and topical information.

Case studies

Jack sets up an online bookstore

Jack lectures in computing in his local community college. To help his students, he has set up an online bookstore on his web site. This bookstore is free and is administered by Amazon, and Jack has listed all the books that his students might need for their studies. As well as providing a safe and convenient service for students, Jack also benefits from the commission he receives on each sale, as an 'affiliate' of Amazon.

Mary's cakes are a credit!

Mary's hobby involves making celebration cakes for weddings, birthdays and the like. These cakes are very popular. Through her internet-surfing son, Mary has spotted a new business opportunity. Since opening an online store through Yahoo!, Mary has sold cakes throughout the United Kingdom as well as one cake to a customer in South Africa.

3 Explaining HTML

In this chapter we will explore:

▶ *the history of HTML*

▶ *setting up an HTML document to launch on the internet*

▶ *adding and formatting text in an HTML document*

▶ *making your text presentable*

▶ *testing HTML documents locally on your PC*

▶ *brightening up your HTML documents*

▶ *adding some advanced formatting functions*

. . . .

The history of HTML

The creator of the world wide web, Tim Berners-Lee, is responsible for HTML (hypertext markup language). He created it to provide a standard method of displaying textual documents on the web. In those early days (1990) HTML was never really visualised as becoming the standard for publishing web documents. However it was such a great little system, with easy to understand commands, that it quickly grew in popularity. HTML is based on an earlier version of a system known as SGML (standard generalised markup language). It has evolved dramatically since its creation in 1990. The current version of HTML is version 4.x.

In a nutshell, an HTML page is a word-processed document with some easy-to-use formatting (tags) added. Here's a very simple example line from an HTML document:

< B >Welcome! < /B >

When the HTML document containing the above line is opened and run (from the web or from your own hard disk), the text will be displayed in bold.

Fig. 22. Bold text in a web page.

Tags are to an HTML document what blood is to a human. The whole concept of designing great web pages reside in your understanding and use of HTML tags. Your complete understanding of HTML will involve the learning of other tags and their operation.

Setting up an HTML document to launch on the internet

In its simplest form, HTML is very easy to create. Unlike more complex programming languages such as Pascal, Delphi or Microsoft Access, it does not require you to purchase a licence, a piece of software, or a set of programming tools. Indeed, you can create HTML on just about any old word processor. If you can use a word processor then you can create HTML. It's that easy.

Once you've created your HTML document using your word processor (Windows 95/98/2000 Notepad, Word, or some other text editor), just save it as a standard text file. Make sure that the file extension is '.htm'. You can then open this file in your favourite browser (e.g. Netscape Navigator or Internet Explorer). There you have it, a working web page.

Using your browser with HTML
In the early days of HTML, its beauty was its simplicity. However this often proved frustrating and limiting, so the two main browsers companies – Netscape and Microsoft – began adding extensions to the HTML language. This caused lots of problems for web designers. For example, if you created an HTML document using the HTML extensions (the name given to any non-standard additions to HTML) in Netscape, and then tried to run this page using Microsoft's Internet Explorer you would get an error (and vice versa). However, this confusion seems to have been sorted, with all the companies now offering more or less standard support for the current versions of HTML.

The official body responsible for setting the standard and developing HTML is the World Wide Web Consortium (W3C). This body has enlisted all the main players to ensure uniformity of use. In this part of the book we'll concentrate on HTML version 3.2. This is a solid version that will run easily on Internet Explorer 3.x and above, and on Netscape Navigator 2.x and above. At the end of the book there's a short chapter on the additions that come with HTML Version 4 (which requires you to have Internet Explorer 4 or Netscape Navigator 4 or above). However, don't worry as with all new software programs, they seem essential but often don't seem that much of an improvement once you have used them for a while.

Create and view a web page in 60 seconds
By following the very simple steps listed below you'll have a web page up and running in no time.

1. Crank up your favourite word processor or open Windows Notepad. Type the following lines in a new document.

```
<HTML>
<HEAD>
<TITLE>Five Second Web Page</TITLE>
</HEAD>
<BODY>
<B>Simple isn't it!</B>
```

```
</BODY>
</HTML>
```

2. Save this document as a simple text file. Use the following filename TEST.HTM (or TEST.HTML if you prefer).

3. Open Internet Explorer, Netscape Navigator or your favourite browser. Choose File, Open and locate and open TEST.HTM (L)

4. Gloat, gloat, your very first web page is now displayed right there on the screen. Well done.

Reviewing the page you've just created
HTML files must include HTML tags. These tags tell your browser that this is a page that will eventually be viewed on the world wide web. All HTML pages follow a similar format:

```
<HTML>
<HEAD>
<TITLE>My first web page</TITLE>
</HEAD>
<BODY>
```

(other HTML stuff in here)

```
</BODY>
</HTML>
<HTML> </HTML>
```

If a document is to be recognised as an HTML document then it must begin and end with these tags. Most tags in HTML are switched on with the tag name itself and switched off with the same tag preceded by a slash (/).

<HEAD> </HEAD>
In this section there's normally only one tag used, the title tag <TITLE>. This allows you to create a page title which is displayed in the Windows Title Bar. For example:

```
<TITLE>This is my first title!</TITLE>
```

Fig. 23. Setting up a title page for your first HTML web page.

The main HTML tags are added within the <BODY> section of the document. This is where you can decide how your document is formatted, and how it appears on the screen when loaded in your browser.

Adding and formatting text in an HTML document

The main purpose of your web page will be to provide information to people who surf there. This information will principally exist in two formats: text and images. Text is therefore the most basic element of your web page and is the best subject to first master using HTML. And guess what – it's all done with tags.

The following HTML tags are the ones most often used to create great formatted text web pages. Even if you never went much further you could present really well-formatted informative text documents on the web by learning not more than half a dozen specific HTML tags.

Creating bold text
Tag: <B> </B>
The bold tag is used before and after any text that you want to display in bold. Figure 24 shows part of a paragraph highlighted in bold. To create the effect, the code shown in figure 25 was used. Note that the area displayed bold in your browser has the <B> at the start of the text to be displayed in bold and the </B> at the end of the text. This ensures that the remaining text in the example reverts back to normal type.

Fig. 24. Example of a web page with some bold text.

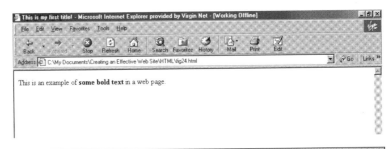

Fig. 25. Using simple HTML tags to create a piece of bold text.

```
File  Edit  Search  Help
<HTML>
<HEAD>
<TITLE>This is my first title!</TITLE>
</HEAD>
<BODY>
This is an example of <B>some bold text</B> in a web page.
</BODY>
</HTML>
```

Creating italic text
Tag: <I> </I>
Creating text in italics helps to emphasise a point and adds interest to your web page. As with making text appear bold, the italics text appears before and after the text being displayed.

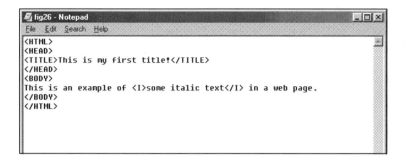

Fig. 26. Using simple HTML tags to create a piece of italic text.

Creating underlined text
Tag: < U > < /U >
Underlining is the third of the most popular formatting tags (the first two being bold and italics). To underline text, you simply place tags around the area of text to be displayed with an underline.

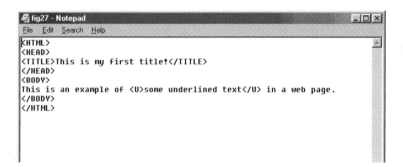

Fig. 27. Using simple HTML tags to underline a piece of text.

Creating subscripts
Tag: < SUB > < /SUB >
Subscripts are used to emphasise an area of text by showing it in a smaller font size than the main text. Subscripts are often used in mathematical, engineering and science web pages to display formulae etc.

Fig. 28. Using simple HTML tags to create some subscript text in a web page.

Creating superscripts
Tag: < SUP > < /SUP >
Superscripts cause text to be shown in a smaller size than the main text and displayed to the top of the line of text being displayed. The most common use of superscript tags is to reference material in a passage. You

might use this, for example, in a web page to show your visitors that the price of an item is listed as published in your most recent catalogue. The following HTML text shows how this might be achieved. When run on a browser, this HTML code would look as shown in figure 30.

Fig. 29. Using simple HTML tags to create some superscript text in a web page.

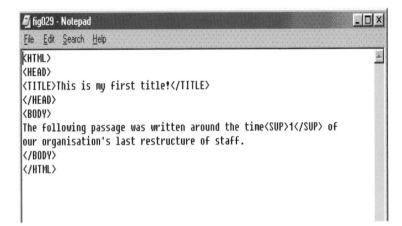

Fig. 30. What the superscript text (created in figure 29) looks like in an actual web page.

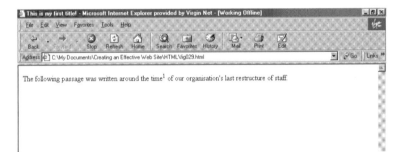

Conquering the scourge of white space

Browsers aren't smart! Things that you might take for granted, such as inserting a tab to create some space between words in your document, cause browsers to have the computer equivalent of a nervous break-down. Don't assume that your browser is smart — that would be a big mistake. You must tell it exactly how to perform and what to do. When loaded, the following line of an HTML document will look as in figure 31.

Now is the   time for all good men to come to the aid of the party.

Fig. 31. Dealing with the problem of white space in HTML.

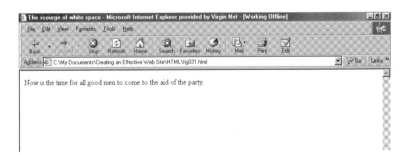

If you just have to display the text the way that you want it to be displayed – after all you are the web site designer– then HTML has a handy little fellow that can help you out. Meet the 'non-breaking space'. or as it's better known: &bnsp. Should you want the above quote to be shown in all its white-space glory (why would you really want to do this?) you would replace the text in the web page with the following:

Now is the   time for all good men to come to the aid of the party.

You can insert as many non-breaking space characters as you wish, each being followed by a semicolon(;).

Inserting special characters
Often, your web pages will require some special characters. The most common one is the copyright symbol . You can use this to let your visitors know that the stuff on the web site belongs to you. The following HTML code is used to add special characters. The table shows the most used characters and their HTML equivalents.

Please ask before using material from this web site. &copy Brendan Murphy 2000.

When viewed in a browser the above HTML code would be displayed as:

Please ask before using material from this web site. © Brendan Murphy 2000.

Special characters:

Character	HTML reference
£	&pound
©	&copy
®	&reg
<	&lt
>	&gt
&	&amp
'	&quote

Displaying preformatted text
Tag: < PRE > < /PRE >
If all the hassle of adding non-breaking spaces seems like a lot of bother, fear not. HTML provides another useful little tag to help. The tag is used to display text in the form in which it was typed. So, for example, if you wanted to display the following just exactly how it looks, then you would use the < PRE > tag:

```
<PRE>
```

Introduction
The History of the Web (Refer App. 1)
Modern ISPs   (Refer App. 2)

```
</PRE>
```

Text formatted using the <PRE> tag often looks a bit out of place on a web page. However, this tag really is useful if the document you wish to publish has lots of centring and white space which might require extensive formatting in HTML – use the <PRE> tag, it's quick and easy.

Mixing and matching
The great news about all this formatting is that it can be interchanged within a web page. The obvious place to mix formatting tags would be in a heading, which might need to be bold, italic and underlined. for example: ***Chapter One***. To achieve this effect on your web page simply use multiple tags at the start and end of the text to be formatted:

<B> <I> <U> Chapter One </U> </I> </B>

Highlighting text with the headings tag
Tag: <H1 > </H1 > to <H6 > </H6 >
HTML comes with a set of preformatted styles, known as headings, which make it easy to emphasise text in a document. These six headings, <H1 > to <H6>, are of varying sizes. <H1 > is the biggest and <H6 > the smallest. Within each heading tag you can set alignment by simply adding an attribute to the tag (this is new!). An attribute is just an extension that allows the tag to perform in a slightly enhanced manner. You put attributes right after the main tag name:

<H4 ALIGN=right> Chapter One </H4 >

In the above example, this attribute would align the heading on the right of the web page. Other alignment options that are available are:

left
center

Making your text presentable

By learning just three more HTML tags you can really develop polished text-based web pages. Try the following tags yourself:

Adding horizontal lines
Tag: <HR >
The <HR > tag is great to split up your page. Simply insert it in your HTML document at a place where you want a horizontal line to appear across the page. This tag also has some useful attributes which add various effects to the line drawn:

<HR WIDTH=percent> – where percent is a percentage value of the screen width

<HR ALIGN=left> (or right or center) – aligns a horizontal line that is not the full width of the screen (used in conjunction with WIDTH).

Changing paragraphs
Tag: <P>
The paragraph tag (<P>) is used to insert a blank line after a paragraph of text in your HTML document. As mentioned earlier, HTML can be a bit funny with line breaks and things, so you sometimes need to give it a hand. Use this tag to create a new paragraph which will include a blank line before it. The paragraph tag also has a great little attribute that will let you align your paragraph text:

<P ALIGN=left> (or right or center)

Forcing a line break
Tag:
It seems that if you can force a new paragraph, then a little brother should exists to allow you to force a new line in your HTML documents. The <BR> tag does this. Place it at any point in your document and the subsequent text appears on a new line.

Checklist for creating an HTML document (web page)
1. Create a new page using Notepad.
2. Make sure you have the correct HTML heading and body structure.
3. Save this new file with either an .HTM or .HTML extension.
4. Add some text in the body of the page and try some of the formatting tags.
5. Save and close.

Testing your HTML web pages locally on your PC

You may think the only way to see whether your HTML masterpiece works properly is to load it on to the internet and surf your way to it. Not so: in fact testing web pages is really very simple.

The page that you've probably just created is stored on your hard disk which is on your personal computer. Make sure you know where it's stored (in what folder) and what it is called (its filename). Whether you're using Netscape Navigator or Internet Explorer as your browser, all you need to do is open your browser and open this newly created file from the File menu just as you would any old word-processed file. Figures 32 and 33 show how to do this in each browser.

Now, simply locate your HTML file from your hard drive and open it. And there you have it all your hard work displayed in your browser just as you intended it and more importantly, just as it would look if loaded onto the internet. Relax and have a coffee!

Fig. 32. How to open an
HTML file if your browser
is Netscape Navigator.

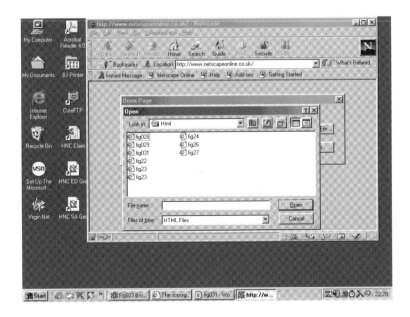

Fig. 33. How to open an
HTML file if your browser
is Internet Explorer.

Brightening up your HTML documents

Remember black and white TV? It was exciting (so my mum told me!) but after a while it became just a little bit dull. Web pages are a bit the same. With all the graphics available on a modern web page it is important to add some life even to straightforward pages. HTML comes with some great colouring tools that allow you to change the colour of both HTML text and page backgrounds. Here's a quick tour of useful tags for you to try. Before that, a word of caution.

Remember your old uncle's tie from the 1970s? Or the album sleeve from your dad's favourite band? Yes, there is such a thing as colour overload. Just as very basic colours can seem flat and dull, so excessive colour changes can end up making your page difficult and hard to read.

Changing your page background colour
Tag: < BODY BGCOLOR='colour value' >
Adding this attribute into the < BODY > tag lets you set a default colour for your page background. When viewed in a browser your page will show the colour chosen. The following table provides a very small list of effective colours that might be used in place of 'colour value'.

Colour	Colour Value
Whitesmoke	#F5F5F5
Springgreen	#00FF7F
Cyan	#00FFFF
Plum	#DDA0DD
Aliceblue	#F0F8FF
Bisque	#FFE4C4
Cornsilk	#FFF8DC
Gold	#FFD700
Ivory	#FFFFF0
Gainsboro	#DCDCDC

For example, to create an ivory background the attribute added to the < BODY > tag would be:

> < BODY BGCOLOR=#FFFFF0 >

Adding colour to text
Tag: < BODY TEXT='colour value' >
Now that you've got a coloured background, why not change the text on your HTML page to match? This attribute allows you to amend the colour of the text on your HTML document. It works in exactly the same way as the BGCOLOR attribute and uses the same colour values.

Changing the colour of some of your text
Tag: < FONT COLOR >
Often you might want to emphasise some text in your HTML document. Changing the colour of a part of the text on the page is a great way of doing this. The < FONT COLOR=colour value > allows you to do this easily. Simply place this tag before the text to be changed. Then, when you wish the text to return to the default, simply end the tag (< /FONT >). The colour value can be any value shown in the table. For example:

> < FONT COLOR=#DDA0DD >This text is now displayed in plum. < /FONT >

This text is displayed in the default text colour for the page.

Changing the default font size of your web page
Tag: < BASEFONT SIZE >
When you create a standard HTML document, the default size of the text on the page is known as 3. This size is normal, and probably equates to a text size of around 12 point. However it may be that you would like the default text size to be larger or smaller than the default. The < BASEFONT SIZE > tag allows you to decide on a font size value between 1 and 7 where 7 is the greatest size and 1 is the smallest size. To use the < BASEFONT SIZE > tag simply insert it as the first line in the body of your HTML document:

```
< BODY >
< BASEFONT SIZE=4 >
```

The main benefit of the < BASEFONT SIZE > tag is that it allows you to change the size of further text in your document relative to the basefont. This means that you could then simply use the < FONT SIZE=-2 > tag to reduce the size of text by a factor of 2 from the value of the basefont. Similarly, using the < FONT SIZE=+1 > would increase the size of text by a factor of 1 from the basefont.

Changing the default font of your web page
Tag: < FONT FACE='Arial, Courier, Tahoma' >
This is a great little tag. It helps to ensure that people viewing your web page from anywhere in the world will see it as you designed it to be seen. In the example shown, this tag will cause a user's browser to firstly try and display the web page in the Arial font. If Arial does not exist on the user's PC, then the rest of the list is tried until a suitable font is found. If none of the fonts listed exist, then your page will be displayed in the default font of the user's browser's preferences.

Adding some moving text
Time to break all the rules. All those smart people who create browsers and other things come up from time to time with really annoying little inventions that make web pages look crazy. However, if you're new to web page design, you may not be able to resist them. The two favourite tags for moving text are:

< MARQUEE > – displays text like the Times Square ticker tape (Internet Explorer only)

< BLINK > – causes text to blink on the screen (Netscape Navigator only)

You decide for yourself. Here's how they work:

< MARQUEE > This text will scroll from right to left < /MARQUEE >

< BLINK > This text will blink and be very annoying! < /BLINK >

Questions and answers

Which browser is best for HTML?
Both of the main browser companies, Netscape (Navigator) and Microsoft (Internet Explorer) offer similar support for HTML, so the choice is up to the individual user.

What's the difference between a word-processed document and an HTML document?
The only difference is that HTML documents have some tags entered which show they are to be read using a standard browser. All HTML documents must be saved in a standard text format, and must have the file extension .htm or .html.

Must HTML tags be in upper-case format?
No. Whether you enter your HTML tags in upper or lower case is immaterial. However, adopting a consistent standard is considered good practice.

Case studies

Anne-Marie creates her first web page.
Anne-Marie is president of her local badminton club. As a keen internet user, she has started putting club fixtures onto the internet. To do this, she simply created HTML documents using Windows Notepad and then transferred these files onto the internet (with help from a friend).

John posts his CV
John has just created an electronic version of his CV. He intends to upload this document onto the internet and invite prospective employers to view it online. He made extensive use of HTML text formatting tags to enhance his CV by including bold, italic and underline areas of text.

Visit the free Internet HelpZone at
www.internet-handbooks.co.uk
Helping you master the internet

---

4 Adding lists and bullets

In this chapter we will explore:

▶ *the benefits of lists in HTML documents*

▶ *creating numbered lists*

▶ *using bullet points to get your message across*

▶ *setting up a glossary of terms using predefined lists*

▶ *adding comments to your HTML documents*

▶ *questions and answers*

▶ *case studies*

. . . .

The benefits of lists in HTML documents

Lists are a great way to add some interest to your web page. Displaying pages of repetitive text on a web site can seem a little boring and unexciting to visitors. These type of pages, as well as looking drab and unappealing, are often quite hard to read on a computer screen. Lists can be used to draw your visitors' attention to a particular point. They can also be used to highlight the steps required to complete a task, or to provide a summary of what has, or what is, to come – just like the list at the top of this page where a bullet list introduces this chapter.

HTML provides three main types of lists:

1. numbered lists
2. bulleted lists
3. definition lists

Creating numbered lists

Using numbered lists to show items in a sequence

Numbered lists provide a great way to place items in order of importance on your web page. This might be your top ten sales items, or your

Fig. 34. Creating a simple numbered list using basic HTML.

```
fig034 - Notepad
File   Edit   Search   Help
<HTML>
<HEAD>
<TITLE>Numbered Lists</TITLE>
</HEAD>
<BODY>
<OL>
<LI>First Item in List
<LI>Second Item in List
<LI>Third Item in List
</OL>
</BODY>
</HTML>
```

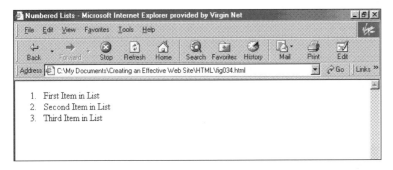

Fig. 35. What the HTML-generated list from figure 34 looks like in an actual web page.

favourite music artists in order of preference. Numbered lists can also used to provide a means of direction to your web site visitors. Maybe you are attempting to list the steps required to make a cake or fix a car brake system – numbered lists show the order (sequence) in which the tasks should be carried out.

Numbered lists are created using the 'ordered list' tag within HTML. Within an ordered list, HTML uses the 'list item' tag to identify each member of the numbered list.

Tag: <OL>, <LI>
Start your numbered list with the <OL> tag. This identifies that an ordered list is to follow. For each item in your list place the <LI> tag at the beginning of each line. Finish you list by using the </OL> tag.

The <OL> tag also has a couple of very useful attributes that add flexibility to your use of numbered lists.

Changing the numbering system used
Tag: <OL TYPE=value> where value is:
A   Each list item will start with capital letters, for example: A, B, C
a   Each list item will start with lower case letters, for example: a,b,c
I   Each list item will start with upper case Roman numerals e.g. I, II, III etc.
i   Each list item will start with lower case Roman numerals e.g. i, ii, iii etc.
1   The list will default to 1, 2, 3 etc.

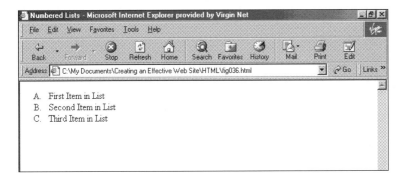

Fig. 36. Using letters to make a list in a web page.

51

Adding lists and bullets ....

Changing the starting number of list items
Tag: < OL START=value > where value is the position in your numbered list that you wish to start from. This attribute is used where you might not want to start your list with the obvious choice of first number e.g.) 1, A, a etc. By making the START attribute default to a different value your list will start at that point in the sequence. If you used the value 'START=5', your list would be numbered from '5' upwards or from 'E' or 'e' or 'V' upwards depending on the TYPE being used.

Fig. 37. Creating an HTML list using the commands TYPE and START.

```
fig037 - Notepad
File  Edit  Search  Help
<HTML>
<HEAD>
<TITLE>Numbered Lists</TITLE>
</HEAD>
<BODY>
<OL TYPE=A START=3>
<LI>First Item in List
<LI>Second Item in List
<LI>Third Item in List
</OL>
</BODY>
</HTML>
```

Using bullet points to get your message across

Numbered lists are great where you want to show items in order, however on many occasions you will want to publish a list but not in any specific order. This type of lists is known as an 'unordered list' or to the average Joe Public a bulleted list. Bulleted list are easy to set up in HTML and are great focus points that help draw attention to a specific part of your web page.

Fig. 38. Creating an HTML unordered list.

```
fig038 - Notepad
File  Edit  Search  Help
<HTML>
<HEAD>
<TITLE>Bulleted Lists</TITLE>
</HEAD>
<BODY>
<UL>
<LI>First Item in List
<LI>Second Item in List
<LI>Third Item in List
</UL>
</BODY>
</HTML>
```

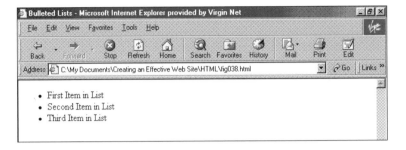

Fig. 39. What an unordered list looks like in an actual web page.

Tag: <UL>, <LI>
Bulleted lists are also known as 'unordered lists.' Bulleted lists start with the <UL> tag. Each item in the list is then preceded by the <LI> tag (the same as in numbered lists). To finish your list, the </UL> tag is used.

Creating a glossary of terms using a definition list

A definition list in HTML is used where you want to give a list of terms, and alongside give a detailed explanation of their meaning. The most common use of this type of list is where you are looking to provide a glossary of terms (similar to the one at the back of this book). Definition lists are a little more complex than numbered and bulleted lists.

TAG: <DL>, <DT>, <DD>
Definition lists start with the <DL> tag with each item in the list having a definition term tag <DT> and an explanation of that definition <DD>. The definition list is terminated with </DL>

Example
    <DL>
    <DT> Apple <DD> A fruit grown on trees in an orchard.
    <DT> Coconut <DD> A Caribbean fruit.
    </DL>

Definition lists display the definition on a separate line from the definition term.

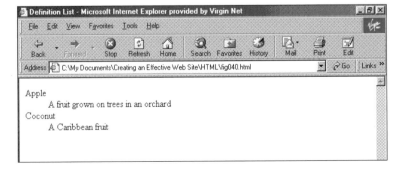

Fig. 40. A definition list in a web page.

Adding lists and bullets ....

Combining ordered, unordered and definition lists
Lists are really useful when designing web pages. However things can really hot up when you combine all the different types of lists. This can result in really professional-looking lists being created.

The following example combines the best of everything you've used in this chapter to create a really effective list.

```
1.  <DL>
2.  <DT>Chapter One<DD>A general introduction to the Internet
3.  <OL>
4.  <LI>ARPANet
5.  <LI>Electronic Mail
6.  <UL>
7.  <LI>Creating a message
8.  <UL>
9.  <LI>E-mail address
10. <LI>Subject
11. <UL>
12. <LI>Choosing an appropriate subject
13. </UL>
14. <LI>Message text
15. </UL>
16. </OL>
17. </DL>
```

In the above HTML code (line-numbered to help you understand) there are three lists:

1. A definition list is shown in lines 1,2 and 17 (where it is completed). This list has only one definition and this refers to the chapter number and name.

2. Within this single item definition list there is a numbered list which describes the many numbered sections of the chapter. This numbered list starts on line 3 and has two items shown on lines 4 and 5. The numbered list finishes on line 16 with the </OL> tag. The item of this numbered list that refers to electronic mail (line 5) is followed by a bulleted list. This list begins on line 6 and ends at line 15.

3. Within this list and under the word 'Subject', a further unordered list displays the phrase 'Choosing an appropriate subject' this simple list begins on line 11 and ends on line 13.

Spend some time looking over the above HTML code until you become familiar with it and understand it fully.

Adding comments to your HTML documents

The above piece of HTML code is quite complex, especially if you're a beginner. Wouldn't it be great if you could include within the HTML document an explanation of what each line of code does? HTML gives you this ability by allowing comments to be placed within HTML documents. These comments can go anywhere in the document and are ignored by browsers which means that you can place any text you like within them. The HTML comments tag is:

<!-- and -->

Example

<!--web page created by B. Murphy, 29 January -->

(No space is allowed between the explanation mark(!) and the first dash(-).)

Questions and answers

Why use lists in HTML documents?
Lists help you create more interesting web pages. They make the page easier to read and less repetitive and they provide a focus to highlight specific points or explain steps in a process.

What type of list would you use to attract visitors to specific points?
You would probably use a bulleted (or unordered) list to attract visitors to important points on your web page.

Case studies

Brian displays his top ten all time favourite records
Brian has set up a personal web site that lists activities and hobbies that interest him. As part of his page, he has decided to include details of his top ten favourite music albums. By using a numbered list in HTML, Brian easily created a list of his favourite music albums.

Theresa makes her point
Theresa is the president of her local school board. To assist board members, she publishes the minutes of monthly meetings on her home page on the internet. To help summarise points, she has used bulleted lists throughout her page to draw attention to the main action points of each meeting.

5 Adding tables

In this chapter we will explore:

▶ *creating simple tables using HTML*

▶ *applying simple formatting techniques to tables*

▶ *applying advanced formatting techniques to tables*

▶ *questions and answers*

▶ *case studies*

. . . .

In the previous chapter we looked at sprucing up HTML documents (or web pages whichever you prefer) by creating lists. Tables are another great way to add interest to your web page.

Creating simple tables using HTML

Tables in HTML are just like those that you might create using a word processor or spreadsheet. They are made up of a set of rows and columns. Each column consists of similar items and each column has a column header. A typical column might contain information such as surnames, forenames or address details. Each row contains a unique item made up of the column information. For example, a typical row of a table might contain the name and address of a particular real-life individual. Each box in the table grid is known as a table cell. In the table shown in figure 41, the name 'Murphy, B' occupies a table cell.

Fig. 41. Using an HTML table to neatly display some names and addresses in a web page.

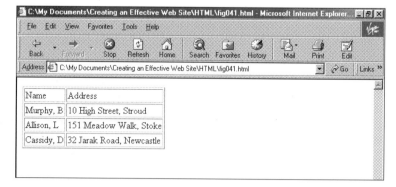

When you create tables in HTML there are lots of other fancy things that can be added, but the above details are all you need to know to start some serious table-building.

Creating simple tables
Tag: < TABLE > < TR > < TD >
Simple tables are just great for simple uses (and often for uses that are not so simple!). So let's get down to business. The following HTML code could be used to create a table giving details of health club opening times:

```
<TABLE>
<TR>
<TD>Monday</TD> <TD>7am-9pm</TD>
</TR>
<TR>
<TD>Tuesday</TD> <TD>7am-10pm</TD>
</TR>
</TABLE>
```

This code seems a bit daunting and only produces the effect in your browser shown in figure 42. However, it does explain the heart of creating great-looking tables.

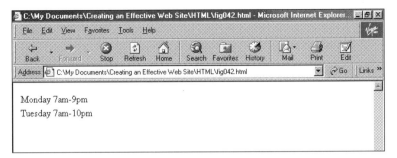

Fig. 42. Laying out some days and times in a web page.

Each table row must be enclosed between <TR> and </TR> tags (<TR>=table row). Every time you include this pair of tags in between the <TABLE> and </TABLE> tags a new row will be created. Within each row you will have a number of columns. Each column is included between <TD> and </TD> tags (<TD> = table data). In the example shown above, there are two columns in each row, one showing the day and the other showing the health club opening times on that day.

Applying simple formatting techniques to tables

The table shown in figure 42 is fine, if rather dull. A good starting point to help liven it up would be to add some column headings and place some lines around the table.

Adding column headings

Column headings help the viewer focus on the contents of each column. In the example, appropriate headings might be 'Day' and 'Opening Times'. To add these headers a new tag is introduced, the table header tag:

Tag: <TH>
This tag is included in the first row of your table. It replaces the column <TD> tags that are used in subsequent table rows. The <TH> tag has a couple of preformatted elements that make it very useful. They automatically ensure that its contents are displayed in bold text, with each word being centred within the table cell. This effect is shown in figures 43 and 44.

57

Adding tables ···

Fig. 43. Adding a header to an HTML table.

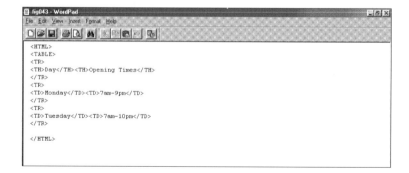

Fig. 44. What the header and HTML table generated in figure 43 look like in an actual web page.

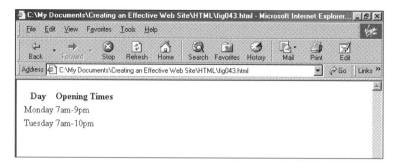

Adding lines around your table

At the moment, the table shown shown in figure 44 is really missing something – you guessed it, lines. When you think of a table you immediately assume that lines should be around every cell. Needless to say, HTML offers a neat way of doing just this: the BORDER attribute.

Tag: <TABLE BORDER=value>

The border attribute is used within the <TABLE> tag. It allows you to specify a value which, when shown in your browser, will display a line of a certain thickness around your table cells. Figures 45 and 46 show a table border of four.

Fig. 45. Using simple HTML to create a table border.

```
<HTML>
<TABLE BORDER=1>
<TR>
<TH>Day</TH><TH>Opening Times</TH>
</TR>
<TR>
<TD>Monday</TD><TD>7am-9pm</TD>
</TR>
<TR>
<TD>Tuesday</TD><TD>7am-10pm</TD>
</TR>

</HTML>
```

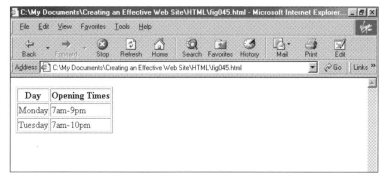

Fig. 46. What the table and border generated in figure 45 look like in a web page.

▶ *Tip* – Values between 1 and 7 create the most effective table borders. Anything bigger than seven starts to look a little out of place when viewed with a browser. Also, remember that changing the thickness of a table border affects only the outline of the entire table. The lines between each cell remain fixed.

Applying advanced formatting techniques to tables

HTML comes with many extras that provide great effects when creating tables. Listed below are the main attributes of the <TABLE> tag which might prove useful to you when designing web pages.

Attribute: ALIGN
This attribute allows you to align a table either left on the page, center or right on the page. This is very useful where text is required to flow around the created table.

Attribute: CELLSPACING=value
This attribute allows you to determine the amount of space between cells in a table. A value between 0 and 5 should suit most table designs.

Attribute: CELLPADDING=value
When you enter data into each cell in each row of a table, the space between the cell data and the lines around the cell can be affected with the cellpadding attribute. Using a value of between 0 and 5 will create varying degrees of white space between the data and the lines in each table cell.

Attribute: COLSPAN
The COLSPAN attribute enables you to merge two or more columns within a table. This is very useful should you require to give some other heading or footer information in your table. Figures 47 and 48 show the added flexibility that HTML offers. The following lines of HTML code (included in the example) help to create a really finished effect:

```
<TR>
<TD COLSPAN=3 ALIGN=center> <B>see club for specific de-
tails</B> </TD>
</TR>
```

Adding tables ....

Fig. 47. Using simple
HTML to specify the
column span of a table.

```
fig047 - Notepad
File  Edit  Search  Help
<HTML>
<HEAD>
<TITLE></TITLE>
</HEAD>
<BODY>
<TABLE border=1>
<TR>
<TH>Day</TH>
<TH>Opening Times</TH>
<TH>Last Entry</TH></TR>
<TR>
<TD>Monday</TD>
<TD>7am-9pm</TD>
<TD>8pm</TD></TR>
<TR>
<TD>Tuesday</TD>
<TD>7am-10pm</TD>
<TD>9pm</TD></TR>
<TR>
<TD COLSPAN=3 ALIGN=center><B>see club for specific details</B></TD>
</TR>
</TABLE>
</BODY>
</HTML>
```

Here, the last row of the table will span three columns. The text entered in
the cell is displayed in a bold face, and centered within the cell.

Fig. 48. What the HTML-
generated table and its
column span look like in an
actual web page.

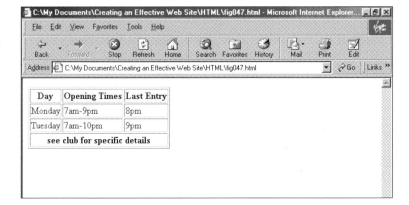

Attribute: ROWSPAN
The ROWSPAN attribute works just like COLSPAN. However, it is used to
merge table rows. This can be useful when you want a left-hand row cell
to cover more than one table row. The HTML document shown in figures
49 and 50 includes the following code:

```
<TR>
<TD ROWSPAN=2>Weekdays & Weekends</TD>
<TD>7am-9pm</TD>
<TD>8pm</TD> </TR>
<TR>
<TD>7am-10pm</TD>
<TD>9pm</TD> </TR>
<TR>
```

60

Notice that the above code shows two rows of your table, indicated by the tags between <TR> and </TR>. In the first row, the ROWSPAN attribute sets the table to merge two rows. The second row in the table has changed from the original table example in that the first column has been removed – the one that said <TD>Tuesday</TD>. This must be done to accommodate the first row's text which, thanks to ROWSPAN, now occupies the table cell space previously occupied by 'Tuesday'. If you forget to do this, just watch the crazy results that can ensue!

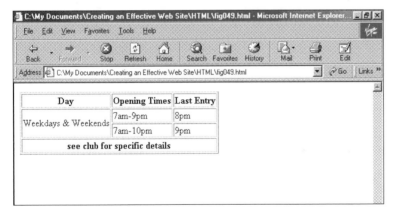

Fig. 49. Using the HTML command, ROWPSAN.

```
fig049 - Notepad
File  Edit  Search  Help
<HTML>
<HEAD>
<TITLE></TITLE>
</HEAD>
<BODY>
<TABLE border=1>
<TR>
<TH>Day</TH>
<TH>Opening Times</TH>
<TH>Last Entry</TH></TR>
<TR>
<TD ROWSPAN=2>Weekdays & Weekends</TD>
<TD>7am-9pm</TD>
<TD>8pm</TD></TR>
<TR>
<TD>7am-10pm</TD>
<TD>9pm</TD></TR>
<TR>
<TD COLSPAN=3 ALIGN=center><B>see club for specific details</B></TD>
</TR>
</TABLE>
</BODY>
</HTML>
```

Fig. 50. What the HTML-generated table and its ROWSPAN look like in a web page.

Day	Opening Times	Last Entry
Weekdays & Weekends	7am-9pm	8pm
	7am-10pm	9pm
see club for specific details		

Attribute: WIDTH=a value or a percentage value

A computer screen is measured in pixels. Pixels are little light-emitting dots that display the image you look at on the screen. Screen definition, or clarity, is determined by the number of pixels used to display the image. A common screen definition would be 600 pixels in height and 800 pixels in width.

The WIDTH attribute allows you to set the maximum width of your table. You can do this either in screen pixels or in a percentage value of the width of the screen. Since you can never be sure what resolution your

61

visitors will have on their PC monitor, it's probably best to use the percentage value here, thus ensuring that your table will look presentable no matter the screen resolution being used.

Attribute: HEIGHT = a value or a percentage value
The HEIGHT attribute determines either the maximum number of pixels in height that your table should occupy on the screen or the maximum percentage height that it should take up.

▶ *Tip* – You should not really use both the WIDTH and HEIGHT attributes unless you have a real need to make your table fit into a defined space. Better to let your browser (and your visitors') take care of table-sizing issues themselves.

Attribute: BGCOLOR
This attribute allows you to determine the background colour of your table. Values include those listed in chapter two.

Attribute: BORDERCOLOR
This attribute allows you to amend the colour of the table border to a specified colour such as those listed in chapter two.

Fig. 51. Using simple HTML to create a smart table.

Putting it all together
Figures 51 and 52 illustrate several the attributes explained above.

```
fig051 - Notepad
File  Edit  Search  Help
<HTML>
<BODY>
<HEAD>
<TITLE></TITLE>
</HEAD>
<BODY>
<TABLE border=1 align=center cellspacing=3 cellpadding=4 width=40%>
<TR>
<TH>Day</TH>
<TH>Opening Times</TH>
<TH>Last Entry</TH></TR>
<TR>
<TD ROWSPAN=2>Weekdays and Weekends</TD>
<TD>7am-9pm</TD>
<TD>8pm</TD></TR>
<TR>
<TD>7am-10pm</TD>
<TD>9pm</TD></TR>
<TR>
<TD COLSPAN=3 ALIGN=center><B>see club for specific details</B></TD>
</TR>
</TABLE>
</BODY>
</HTML>
```

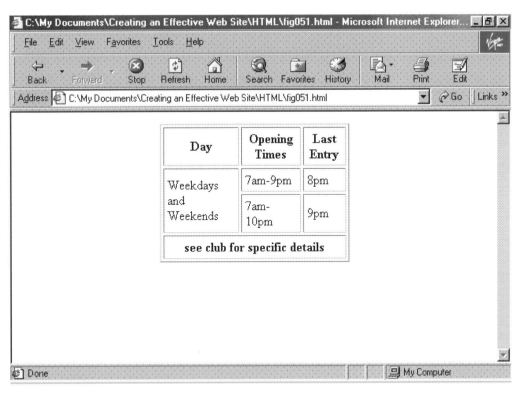

Fig. 52. What the HTML-generated smart table looks like in an actual web page.

Questions and answers

What is the point of using the cellpadding attribute?
The cellpadding attribute creates a wider area of white space between the data in your cell and the border around it. By increasing the cellpadding value, your tables can be made to look less cluttered and less tightly packed.

When would I use the table width attribute?
The table width attribute lets you define the exact width that a table will occupy in the browser window. By defining it in percentage terms you can ensure that your web page will look similar no matter what browser or screen definition is used.

Case studies

Stephen's currency converter
Stephen has a holiday home in San Juan in southern Spain. At work, he is the expert on everything Spanish. To help his colleagues (and to reduce the amount of questions he has to answer over the summer months), Stephen has set up an HTML table giving currency conversion for standard amounts of British pounds. His colleagues can now visit his web site to see what any particular amount of sterling is worth in pesetas or euros.

Adding tables ....

Carol's price list

Carol runs a successful butcher's business that exclusively supplies the catering trade. She has just finished creating her first web page for the business and has decided to include a price list of all her meat products. Using HTML tables, Carol has easily set this up. To present the price list more attractively, she has increased the border size to make the table stand out. She has also changed the background colour of the table from grey to light green to add further definition and brighten up her visitors' experience when visiting her site.

6 Adding graphic images, animation and sounds

In this chapter we will explore:

▶ *graphic images and files*

▶ *adding graphics images to your web site*

▶ *more graphic image formats*

▶ *some free graphic image sites*

▶ *adding background sounds to your web site*

▶ *some free music sites*

▶ *adding other smart stuff to your web site*

▶ *questions and answers*

▶ *case studies*

Graphic images and files

If you've spent any time looking around the internet you will have seen an amazing array of pictures, and photographs on various web sites. Apart from particularly academic or technical sites, most sites have a high graphic content. To add graphic images to your web site is relatively straightforward (once you've actually got the graphic image file you wish to add) and will add great appeal and professionalism to your site. However, a word of caution. You really can get 'too much of a good thing', especially on the world wide web. Large graphic image files take time to load and in a couple of seconds your visitors may decide surf to some-where that's quicker to load. When designing web pages it's very easy to forget that your visitors' hardware and software might not be as up to date as yours, therefore their view of your site might be slower and different.

Explaining file types
The whole area of personal computing and in particular Windows and the internet has created a whole industry built around graphic images. Graphic image files come in all sorts of shapes and sizes and usually come shrouded in much technical jargon and intrigue. This has the unfor-tunate effect of putting people off experimenting and trying things for themselves.

In essence, you will use two types of graphic image file when creating your web pages. These are:

GIF files
JPG or (JPEG) files

Adding graphic images, animation and sounds......................

GIF files

GIF stands for 'graphics interchange format'. It refers to the graphics that you will mostly come across on the web. The chances are that 80% of the graphics on any web page you choose to view will be GIF files. GIF files are compressed and are great for displaying clipart and other images that have a lot of single colours, such as drawings, maps or country flags. GIF files are restricted to 256 colours. This means that they are not completely at home with images that require a wider range of colours. If you look around the web in some of the sites listed later in this chapter you'll find plenty of GIF images that can be downloaded and added to your web site.

JPEG files

JPEG stands for 'joint photographic experts group'. JPEG files are often known as JPGs as well as JPEGs. This file type is great for images that have colours that fade and blend like a photograph where it's harder to define an exact colour. When adding graphic images to your web site, all photographs – whether taken with a digital camera or scanned using a scanner – are likely to be JPEG file types. JPEG files can be compressed better than GIF files. If your web site is to contain lots of graphic images, this might be an issue worth considering.

Checklist for choosing a graphic image format
1. Use GIF format for clipart.
2. Use JPEG format for photographs (nearly 100% quality is achieved).
3. Remember that JPEGs are smaller than GIFs and will therefore load more quickly.
4. JPEGs load from the top line of the image to the bottom, so can seem to be slow.
5. GIFs fade into view (known as 'interlacing').
6. Practise and decide yourself what looks best.

Adding graphic images to your HTML document

The image tag

Tag: < IMG SRC='filename.gif' or 'filename.jpg' >

Place the image tag in the exact place where you want the graphic to appear in your HTML document (figure 53). This way your image will be displayed when you view your document in your browser (figure 54). The 'IMG' denotes that an image is being displayed, the 'SRC' determines where it is stored and 'filename' is the name of the image being displayed.

Fig. 53. Using simple HTML to insert an image into a web page.

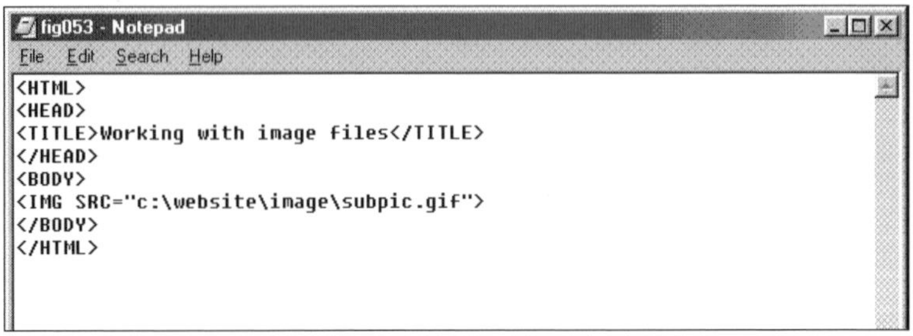

```
fig053 - Notepad
File  Edit  Search  Help
<HTML>
<HEAD>
<TITLE>Working with image files</TITLE>
</HEAD>
<BODY>
<IMG SRC="c:\website\image\subpic.gif">
</BODY>
</HTML>
```

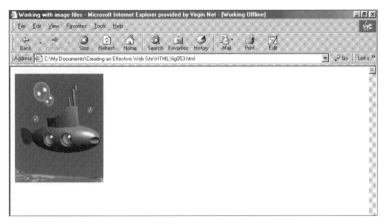

Fig. 54. What the HTML-inserted image looks like in a web page.

Storing images

If you're used to creating folders and sub-folders in Windows Explorer or DOS, then you might consider splitting the elements (files and images) of your web site into different storage areas on your hard disk. However when you load pages onto the internet it's a whole lot easier to keep everything in the same folder. However, should you be loading a graphic image that isn't in the current folder or sub-folder, remember to point to the area that it's stored in. The following examples show a GIF file loading from a specific sub-directory on a PC hard disc:

< IMG SRC='c:/website/image/logo.gif' >

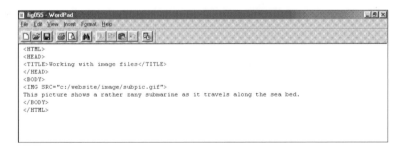

Fig. 55. Specifying an HTML paragraph with a GIF image of a submarine.

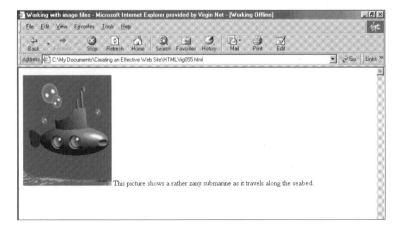

Fig. 56. What the submarine image looks like in a web page, with the HTML paragraphing specification.

67

Adding graphic images, animation and sounds......................

Fig. 57. Writing an HTML paragraph to adjust the alignment of text and image.

```
File   Edit   Search   Help
<HTML>
<HEAD>
<TITLE>Working with image files</TITLE>
</HEAD>
<BODY>
<IMG SRC="c:/website/image/subpic.gif" ALIGN=middle>
This picture shows a rather zany submarine as it travels along the sea
</BODY>
</HTML>
```

In figures 55 and 57, the path for the graphic image file is referenced using forward slashes to determine the pathname ('c:/website/image/logo.gif'). The reason is that, when any web page that contains a graphic image is uploaded onto the world wide web for all to visit, you will be required to reference each graphic image file in a similar format. A typical graphic image file, already loaded onto the world wide web, might look something like the following:

< IMG SRC='http://vzone.virgin.net/jack.smorton/logo.gif

Aligning text around graphic images
Once you've inserted your graphic image into your HTML document you'll notice some problems with the text displayed around the image. This alignment problem can be easily rectified by using the ALIGN attribute with the <IMG> tag. This offers you up to nine different ways of aligning text around graphic images (figure 57).

ALIGN=left – The image will be displayed in the left margin with subsequent text wrapping to the right of the image.

ALIGN=right – The image will be displayed in the right margin with subsequent text wrapping to the left of the image.

ALIGN=top – The image will align itself with the top of the tallest item on the line where it is placed.

ALIGN=texttop – The image will align itself with the top of the tallest text on the line where it is placed.

ALIGN=middle – The text around the image will be displayed with the bottom of the text being placed in the middle of the image.

ALIGN=absmiddle – The text around the image will be aligned with the middle of the text being placed in the middle of the image.

ALIGN=baseline – The bottom of the image will be aligned with the bottom of the text (baseline) on the line.

ALIGN=bottom – The bottom of the image will be aligned with the baseline of the current line.

ALIGN=absbottom – The image will be aligned with the bottom of the current line.

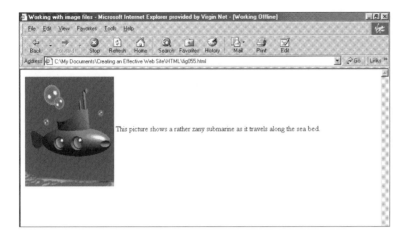

Fig. 58. What the submarine image and text look like aligned in a web page.

Spend some time experimenting with the various alignment methods available.

Adding an image to your web page background
The BACKGROUND attribute can be used to point to an image file that will be tiled across the browser window, to provide a background for the web page being displayed.

< BODY BACKGROUND='filename.gif' >

The above attribute, used with the < BODY > tag, will ensure that the GIF file included would be displayed on the background of the browser window, tiled to fit the complete window.

Ensuring everyone can deal with images
Whilst the vast majority of visitors to your site will use either Internet Explorer or Netscape Navigator as their browser you must also consider those that choose to use either a different browser or a very old browser. The < IMG > tag comes with a very useful attribute that will display a message where the image should be displayed for those who can't successfully display images.

ATTRIBUTE: ALT='message text to be displayed in place of image'

Example
< IMG SRC='dog.gif' ALT='A picture of a dog' >

▶ *Tip* – Some people will choose to disable the viewing of images in their browser (this is done by accessing a menu option in the browser software). This speeds up their use of the internet as no large graphic image files will be downloaded to view. This way people cut down on expensive telephone charges and long site loading delays.

69

Adding graphic images, animation and sounds......................

More image formats

It's worth mentioning the other formats that can be used on the web and which you are sure to come across, namely 'bitmapped files' and 'animated GIFs'.

BMP files
BMP or 'bitmapped files' have been around for a long time. Indeed, they were the de facto standard in the early days of Windows. These files can easily be loaded onto the web, but they tend to be large, and slow for browsers to load, so it's better to convert them to GIF or JPEG format before adding them to your site.

Animated GIFs
Animated GIFs are a fancy version of the standard GIF file. This format enables GIFs to display animated characteristics. Remember the old pack of cards with the dancing clown? Each card showed the clown in a slightly different position, giving you the effect of movement when you held one end of the cards tightly in one hand and used the thumb of the other hand to ruffle the open end whilst viewing the images. Animated GIFs work in much the same way. A number of slightly different GIF images are combined into one GIF image which displays sequentially, creating an illusion of movement. Creating animated GIFs is probably better left until you have a full understanding of web site development. The good news is that the internet has many sites packed with downloadable free animated graphics. Animated GIFs are used just like normal GIF files, using the < IMG > tag.

Converting graphic image files
Sooner or later, when working with image files, you'll want to convert a

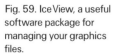
Fig. 59. IceView, a useful software package for managing your graphics files.

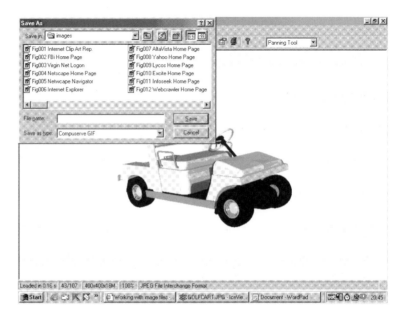

GIF to a JPEG or a BMP to a GIF or some other combination. To do this you'll need a graphics package that will allow you to save your files in different formats. Two of the best on the web are:

IceView

GIFConstructionSet

Both these provide comprehensive facilities to create and modify graphic images ready to be added to your web site. Both packages are shareware and require you to pay a small amount of money (around £15 to £20) should you decide to continue using them.

In IceView, to save an image in a different format simply open the image file and save as the required format (see figure 59).

Some free graphic image sites

Visit the following sites and download images to use in your HTML documents:

Animation Factory
http://www.animfactory.com
This site has a wealth of animated GIF files. With over 12,000 images to choose from, in some 200 categories, you can't fail to find the right images for your web site. The site also has an 'animation of the day' plus a description on the home page of new releases to the site. You can also buy a CD of 30,000 animations if you think that you might be making extensive use of the site contents. This site also has some good online tools for creating buttons and banners to use on your web site. An all-round fantastic site – satisfaction guaranteed.

GIFArt.com
http://www.gifart.com
GIFArt.com offers you a choice from around 10,000 graphic images. It has all the usual categories of buttons and backgrounds that you might expect, as well as an area where more unusual images exist. It also provides links to other graphic image sites and web page tutorial and help sites. The popularity and success of this site can be seen by the number of internet awards it has notched up.

Clipart.com
http://www.clipart.com
Clipart.com is a great source from which to start looking at free graphic image sites on the web. Apart from providing a comprehensive list of free images it also provides links to all the most visited graphics sites on the internet.

ArtToday
http://www.arttoday.com
ArtToday offers visitors either a paid or free subscription. You might wonder about the benefit of paying for this site when you realise that

Adding graphic images, animation and sounds.......................

free membership gives you access to over 40,000 web graphic images.

GraphicsFreebies.com
http://www.graphicsfreebies.com
This site offers visitors the chance to add their own graphic image site to the site owners 'chart'. Visitors can then vote for your site and this is shown in a league table within GraphicsFreebies. This is a good way to see the graphics sites on the web that are receiving the most visits. There is no better measurement of the usefulness of a site than the number of visitors it attracts. Look around the top five sites and you're sure to find many wonderful images ready for use.

Downloading images direct from web sites
As you surf the world wide web you're sure to notice some eye-catching graphic images, most of which can be downloaded by placing your mouse cursor over the image, right-clicking, and choosing 'Save Picture As' (see figure 60). The file can then be saved on your PC and used just as any other image file.

Fig. 60. Saving an image from a web site. Right-clicking your mouse produces the pop-up menu. Then click on 'Save picture as' to store it on your computer.

Observing copyright
Please remember that, whilst it is very easy to grab images straight from the web, there may be an issue of copyright. The web is made up of philosophical, cool, laid back individuals who may be quite happy for you to use images found on their web site (this won't include the IBMs

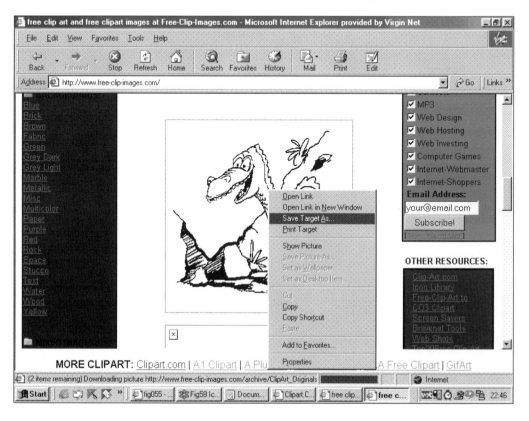

72

and Coca Colas of this world). Please respect people's intellectual right to property. If you're going to use a graphic image, send an email to the site owner and get the appropriate permission. The commercial sites listed will give details of copyright and this will usually simply require you to either make reference or add a link to their site.

Optimising your graphic images for use
When you create your web site, full of images, and you test it on your super-fast Pentium PC, you'll probably find that everything works well and your pages are displayed at lightning speed. However, remember that the web is world wide, and its beauty is its diversity. There are plenty of people out there with slow machines, slow browsers and slow modems. How can you be sure that everything will work at an acceptable speed?

When using graphic images in your HTML document, you can employ an 'optimiser' that will ensure that your images are in the best format for the wider internet community. Some of the packages you used to create and manipulate images may include optimiser units. However, a very useful option exists at Website Garage:

Website Garage
http://www.websitegarage.com
Here, you can submit your page through the GIFLube utility (figure 61) and have it optimised for you. Optimising images on your web site should increase the appeal and speed of loading of your site.

Fig. 61. The GIF Lube browser page, run by Website Garage. You can use their service to compress your images so they load more quickly on your own web page.

Adding background sounds to your web site

Adding music and sounds to your web site is a great way of conveying the general feeling of the site. Visitors will quickly get an understanding of what they have entered depending on the music or sounds used. For

Adding graphic images, animation and sounds......................

example classical music on entry will convey a very different meaning from hip hop which in turn would give a different feel to the gentle tweeting of wild birds. Whilst sounds can really enhance a web page, after a while they can also become a bit tedious. Therefore it's important to include a switch to allow visitors to switch the sound off.

Sound file types
Similar to graphics, sound on the web comes in many formats. The three main file types that you will come across are: WAV, AU and MIDI, and the new kid on the block, MP3.

▶ *WAV files* – This are by far the most common sound file format on the internet. They can be played by most PCs running Windows95, Windows98 or Windows2000 and are understood by the two most popular browsers, Netscape Navigator and Internet Explorer.

▶ *AU files* – These 'audio' files are commonly used on UNIX based machines. They are also used in more advanced web design tools such as Java.

▶ *MIDI files* – Musical instrument digital interface, or 'MIDI' file format, is popular with synthezisers. If you've got a synth and want to compose and link your musical masterpiece to your PC then this is the format to use. MIDI file resources are becoming more and more popular on the internet due to their rich sound quality. It is now perfectly acceptable to use them in your web site.

▶ *MP3* – MP3 files can be entire songs, words and sounds. They are compressed into small files that can be downloaded fairly quickly from the internet. For the moment the main use of this file format is to load it onto a special media player (just like a Sony Walkman) which allows you to listen to the downloaded music. This form of music purchase could become the norm in the future where, instead of purchasing CDs from your local record store, you would download them from the internet.

Choosing a sound file type
Don't worry about all the fancy file types listed above – just like the spaghetti junction of file types available for images used on the Internet, clear leaders appear. For the foreseeable future the WAV and MIDI formats will be king.

Inserting background sound into your HTML document
To insert a piece of music into your web site requires a very simple tag:

TAG: < BGSOUND >

This HTML tag appears in the following form:

< BGSOUND SRC='filename.wav' or 'filename.mid' >

where SRC refers to the file path and 'filename.wav/midi' refers to the

WAV/MIDI file to be played.
  This tag also has a very useful attribute: LOOP:

  < BGSOUND SRC='filename.wav' LOOP=value >

In the above, 'value' can be any number starting from 1 and reaching INFINITE for continuous play.

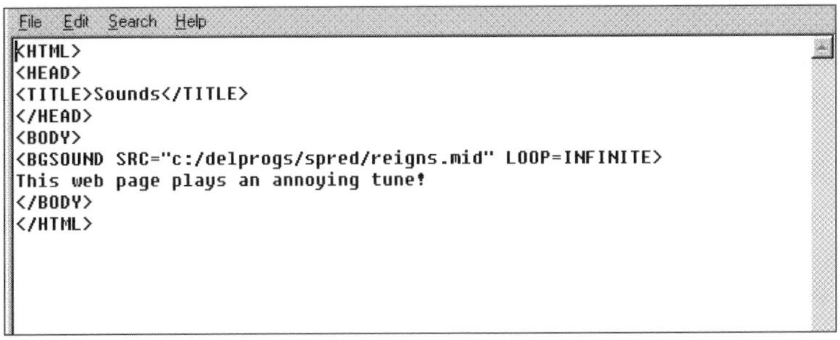

```
File  Edit  Search  Help
<HTML>
<HEAD>
<TITLE>Sounds</TITLE>
</HEAD>
<BODY>
<BGSOUND SRC="c:/delprogs/spred/reigns.mid" LOOP=INFINITE>
This web page plays an annoying tune!
</BODY>
</HTML>
```

Fig. 62. Some simple HTML to insert an infinite music loop into your web page.

Note: < BGSOUND > only works with Internet Explorer.

Some free music sites
The following sites should contain a wide enough range of music files to have your web site playing and singing its little heart out!

Wavhounds.com
http://www.wavhounds.com
The people at Wavehounds seem to have a fixation on rude sounds in WAV format. So if you're interested in bodily functions or the sound of vomiting then this is the site for you. On the serious side, Wavhounds also has a comprehensive search engine that links to more acceptable WAV format files.

The Daily WAV
http://www.dailywav.com
The Daily WAV provides a great archive of WAV files. Simply choose an archive letter of the alphabet and listen to some cool sounds made by such maestros as Johnny Depp, Burt Ward (famed for playing Robin in the original Batman series) and John Hurt. This site also has, as the name suggests, a daily downloadable WAV file, e.g. 'Watch out Batman, this could be tricky' – great fun!

The Movie Sound Database
http://www.geocities.com/Hollywood/Theater/6219/
If you fancy adding the theme from *The Dambusters* to your web site take a look at this site. It has lots of movie WAV files to make your web page seem perform like something straight out of the movies.

Adding graphic images, animation and sounds.....................

Xiang
http://listen.to/midipalace
'Xiang' means 'noise' in Chinese. Visit this site to find lots of MIDI files that cover a wide range of music tastes. You'll find theme tunes, classical music, popular, oldies, new age and even hymns at this site.

Valkhorn
http://www.all-midi.net/valkhorn/
This site has a comprehensive source of over 20,000 MIDI files. Some interesting categories include Big Band, National Anthems and Bluegrass music.

Adding other smart stuff to your web site

Developing a marquee
In the last chapter we looked at adding a 'marquee'. A marquee is a piece of scrolling text that moves across your screen like the electronic ticker tape in Times Square, Manhattan. Now, lets consider the full advantage and usage that this tag might bring to your web page. The MARQUEE tag is great for drawing attention to site updates, or special information such as a sale, or extended opening times or a reminder to register for a new club membership. The following attributes really bring it alive:

1. BGCOLOR = value. This attribute changes the background colour of the < MARQUEE >. Values include all those set out in Appendix One.

2. DIRECTION = LEFT or RIGHT. This attribute allows you to determine whether your text within the < MARQUEE > will scroll from the left or the right of the screen. The default value will see your text scroll from right to left.

3. ALIGN = value. This attribute allows you to determine how the text around the < MARQUEE > will align. Values can be either TOP, MIDDLE or BOTTOM (just like the TV show!) and this determines whether the surrounding text will align with the top of the < MARQUEE >, its middle or its bottom.

4. BEHAVIOR = SCROLL or SLIDE or ALTERNATE. This attribute allows you to determine the behaviour of your text within the < MARQUEE >. SCROLL will see the text appear within the < MARQUEE > pass through it and move completely off the screen this sequence will then repeat. SLIDE sees your text scroll from one side and stop as soon as the text touches the other side of the < MARQUEE >. ALTERNATE will see your text bounce about within the < MARQUEE >.

5. LOOP = value. This attribute can have a value from 1 to INFINITE and this determines the number of times that the < MARQUEE > text will roll. Good practice, and something that will stop your visitors putting their fists through their PC screens, suggests that a scroll of three or four times should be sufficient to attract attention. Use the INFINITE

value on pages where the information really needs to be displayed continuously.

There are many other ways to make your web site sing and dance. You can add video, have your page perform magical animations, have a 360° view of your workplace or home as well as including many other animated and 3-D effects. All of these effects require you to look a bit further into the issues surrounding web site development. Listed below are the main technologies that you should consider looking at.

CU-SeeMe
http://www.wpine.com/Products/CU-SeeMe-Pro/Index.html
CU-SeeMe ('see you, see me') is a fantastic product that lets you communicate in near real-time across the internet (or company intranet). Links are maintained in full colour and have excellent audio abilities. By simply setting up your PC with the right software and a multimedia kit (speakers, microphone and in some cases a web camera) you can see and hear relatives and associates from around the world with calls costing the price of a local phone call.

QuickTime
http://www.apple.com/quicktime/
QuickTime allows you to play digitised video, audio and virtual reality movies. The package comes as a freely downloadable viewer which will allow you to play files created by someone else (or on another web site when your surfing) or as a commercially available inexpensive package that will allow you to create and edit your own movies. QuickTime is particularly good when you want to create 360° views of a building or place of interest and can be set up to allow hotspots that allow you to move through a building giving you the feeling of virtual reality.

RealPlayer
http://www.real.com
RealPlayer is becoming extremely popular with many major TV and radio companies as it allows streamed audio and video to be played over the internet. Streaming refers to the process whereby a file is opened and played as it's being downloaded from the internet. Normally you would expect to download the file first and then play it through a piece of software like Microsoft's Media Player. However RealPlayer opens the file as it arrives giving an almost instantaneous play back. It comes with an excellent front end that incorporates channels, which are similar to TV and radio receivers, and you can easily tune and listen to your favourite station. To use RealPlayer you need a fast modem, probably 56K.

Shockwave Player
http://www.macromedia.com
Shockwave player is what makes all those web pages look professional. It allows for the inclusion of very rich multimedia playback in web pages and is widely used on the major sites.

Adding graphic images, animation and sounds.......................

Microsoft NetMeeting
http://www.microsoft.com/netmeeting/
NetMeeting allows you to communicate with family, friends and colleagues all over the world. You have the choice of using text messages, chatting in real time, conducting an actual audio conversation or creating a video link (if you have a web camera).

Understanding plug-ins
The things we've talked about above are commonly known as 'plug-ins'. A plug-in is a piece of software added to your browser to enhance your web design and surfing capabilities. Yet if you spend a little time mastering all the basics of sound and images you'll end up with really snazzy pages without having to spend any time understanding these complex software packages. Maybe when you are ready, you can spend some time looking at each package in turn and determine the best one to suit your needs.

Questions and answers

What's the best graphic image file type to use on my web site?
The two main file types use to display graphic images are GIF and JPG formats. As a general rule of thumb, you should use GIFs for drawings and clipart and JPG for photographs.

How can I ensure that my web site will load quickly in a number of browsers?
You can ensure that your web site is tuned up and ready to go by running it through a web site checker. A site such as http://www.websitegarage.com will check your web pages for conformity to good HTML design, quick loading of graphic images and compatibility with a range of browser versions.

Case studies

Martin gets wired for sound
Martin has recently added a bank of background music to his web pages. Whilst he was really pleased with his efforts, his friends who have been visiting his site suggested that he only plays each piece of music once, because after surfing his site for more than five minutes they were getting a headache.

Morag's family online
Morag has a large extended family in Canada, Florida USA, Australia and New Zealand. Since she has always felt close to her relatives she has recently added a 'picture gallery' to her web site where she loads images taken using her digital camera. Her extended family around the world can now keep up to date with the activities and adventures of her two sons at home.

7 Getting feedback

In this chapter we will explore:

▶ *getting visitor feedback by email*
▶ *creating visitor feedback forms*
▶ *adding a visitor counter to your web site*

. . . .

Getting visitor feedback by email

Visitors to your web site will probably have two main reasons for stopping by. Firstly, they may want to find out about you, your club, organisation or business, with a view to contacting you. Secondly, they'll want to do just that, contact you. By adding some simple extensions to your web site you can enable visitors to contact you either by email, or by completing a form which sits as an HTML document on your web site.

Using the 'mailto:' attribute
The 'mailto:' attribute is used as part of the anchor <A> tag in HTML. The anchor tag is used when you want to create a hypertext link within your web site. A hypertext link, when clicked, transfers the user either to another place on the current web page, or to another page in the current site, or to another web site altogether. The 'mailto:' attribute allows visitors to your site to send you an email message.

The following piece of HTML code illustrates how the 'mailto:' attribute is used:

Contact me at: <A HREF="mailto:brendan.murphy@virgin.net"> brendan.murphy@virgin.net</A>

Consider the above example. By clicking on brendan.murphy@virgin.net, the visitor's browser software will automatically load the default mail software being used on their PC (probably Outlook Express if they are using Internet Explorer). Their software will also complete the email address of the recipient of the email message with the address shown in the anchor <A> tag. The visitor can then complete the subject and email contents, and send a message as normal. You will then receive the message through your normal email software. The 'HREF' element turns the text between the opening <A> and closing </A> into hypertext.

Fig. 63. Using HTML to insert an email reply form on your web site, using the 'mailto' command.

Getting feedback ....

Using 'mailto:' is a good way of enabling visitors to your site to make general enquiries. However, should you want a more structured enquiry to be completed, there is another method of obtaining web site feedback.

Creating visitor feedback forms

The commonest use of forms in basic web sites is a 'visitors book.' A typical book might look like figure 64.

Fig. 64. An example of a feedback form on a web site (in this case, of the UK internet service provider Freeserve).

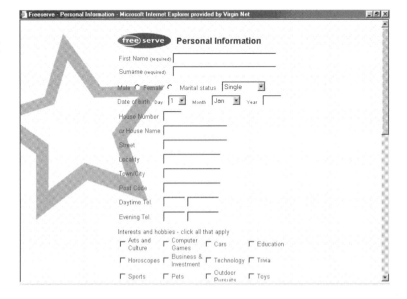

Creating a simple data entry form
Tag: < FORM >
By placing the following tags in your HTML document you create an area where users can enter useful information:

< FORM ACTION='url'.METHOD=POST > </FORM>

The ACTION attribute tells the web page what to do with the information that the user enters onto the form. Most ISPs provide a 'CGI program' to enable you to make sense of the information gathered on your form.

CGI programs
CGI stands for common gateway interface. It is the method used to transfer the information gathered on your form, from the server it is held on, to a CGI program able to process it. CGI programs are very difficult to write and are not covered in this book.

However, the good news is that your ISP will almost certainly let you have a CGI program which can be used to make sense of information gathered on your web site forms (if they don't, then consider changing your ISP.) Use of these CGI programs is free. If you look around your ISP's home page, you should find details on how to use them.

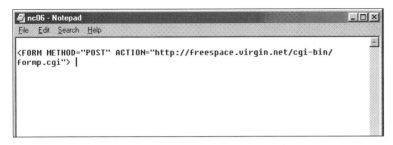

Fig. 65. Writing some simple HTML to place a Virgin CGI Form program on your web site.

By placing the CGI program reference provided by your ISP into the URL attribute of the <FORM> tag, the details gathered on your form are processed and sent back to you as an email message. Figure 65, for example, shows Virgin Net's CGI program reference for forms.

The 'METHOD=POST' attribute tells the browser how you want to send the information gathered on your form to the web site identified in the ACTION attribute. The only method that you need to use is 'POST'.

So, to complete the opening part of your form you should end up with something like this:

< FORM METHOD = 'POST' ACTION = http://www.ispname.com/ cgi-bin/forms.cgi >

Alternative form processing
Using CGI programs is by far the best way to process web site form information, but you can also make use of the <MAILTO> tag. This is fine where your form has only a limited amount of information to be gathered. The <MAILTO> attribute used within a FORM sends the completed form back to your email address as one long line of text. This creates the problem of how to easily identify the information gathered.

< FORM METHOD = 'POST' ACTION = mailto:brendan.murphy@ virgin.net >

Fig. 66. Creating a form with eight fields for your web site. The fields are title, forename, surname, email, web site, country, comments, and send more information.

Getting feedback ....

Adding fields to your form

A field is a category of information. It's the sort of information that you need to gather from the form completed by your web site visitors. Typical fields would be forename, surname, title, and age. To add fields to your form, use the <INPUT> tag. Figure 66 illustrates the addition of eight fields. The first field in the form 'Title' shows the use of a selection box.

```
< SELECT NAME='Title' >
< OPTION > Not Known
< OPTION > Mr.
< OPTION > Mrs.
< OPTION > Miss
< OPTION > Ms.
< OPTION > Dr.
< OPTION > Rev.
< /SELECT >
```

Here, the user can choose from a list of available titles. If no title is chosen, the default information that will be returned to you will be the first entry in the list (hence use of the 'not known' entry)

The next three fields, 'forename', 'surname' and 'email address' are examples of the simplest and most commonly used field on a form, namely input fields.

```
< INPUT TYPE=TEXT NAME='Forename' >
```

The <INPUT> tag has an attribute 'TYPE'. This allows you to add variety to your form fields.

Since all web addresses start with the term 'http://' - and usually follow with 'www.' - you can set some defaults within your form to help visitors completing it.

```
< INPUT TYPE=TEXT NAME='Web site address' VALUE 'http://
www.' >
```

In the example shown, your visitors are required to enter which country they live in. This is achieved by using the 'RADIO' attribute of the <INPUT> tag:

```
< INPUT TYPE=RADIO NAME='Country' VALUE 'Scotland' >
   Scotland < BR >
< INPUT TYPE=RADIO NAME='Country' VALUE 'England' >
   England < BR >
< INPUT TYPE=RADIO NAME='Country' VALUE 'Ireland' >
   Ireland < BR >
< INPUT TYPE=RADIO NAME='Country' VALUE 'Wales' >
   Wales < BR >
```

When visitors complete your form they will only be able to select one of the radio buttons shown. By naming all the radio buttons as 'country', the email message returned to you when the form is completed will include the appropriate country name entered by your web site visitors.

Most forms you create for your web site will have a 'free text' area. Here, visitors can request information or make a comment. Creating this type of field within a form requires use of the <TEXTAREA> tag.

<TEXTAREA NAME='Comments' ROWS=4 COLS=40> </TEXTAREA>

In the above example your visitors will be able to add comments up to four rows long, with a maximum of 40 characters per row.

In the final field of the form illustrated, visitors have the option to request further information. This is best done using a checkbox. A checkbox is just a one-character box that toggles between a tick and a blank when clicked with the mouse.

<INPUT TYPE=CHECKBOX NAME='Send Info'> Send more information

Sending form information or starting from scratch
Once your web site visitors have completed the details required on the form, they will do one of two things: send the form to you, or make some changes to it. Most forms you see on web sites have two buttons at the bottom of the form, to facilitate these two activities. They are the 'submit' and 'reset' buttons. Again, it's quite simple to include them in your forms:

   <INPUT TYPE=SUBMIT VALUE='Send'>
   <INPUT TYPE=RESET VALUE='Clear Form'>

If the 'submit' button is pressed, the details gathered on your form are sent off to be emailed to you. They end up looking something like figure 67.

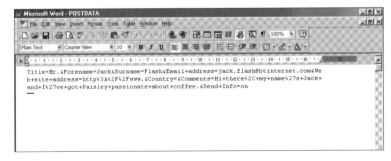

Fig. 67. This is how information looks when gathered from someone using a form, ready for emailing back to you.

If the 'reset' button is selected, the form fields are cleared allowing visitors to recomplete the form. You can choose the most appropriate 'labels' to place on your buttons and these can replace the words 'Send' and 'Clear Form'.

▶ *Note* – The fields in each form are returned to you on separate lines within the email, with each line beginning with the field name. This name is determined by the value that you place in the NAME attribute of each field.

Getting feedback ··

Formatting forms

When you create forms using HTML, the alignment of each field can be a problem. You can ensure alignment of fields by using the ' ' character between the text describing the field and the form field itself. You could also place your form in a two-column table with the left column holding the field text and the right column the form tags and attributes.

Fig. 68. An example of a web site (called Hotel Room) which includes a counter. According to the counter, the site has been visited 525,515 times since 22nd January 1997.

Adding a visitor counter to your web site

Counters are the commonest method of telling how many people have visited your web site. Most of the commercial and personal web sites that you see on the world wide web include a counter. Developing a counter yourself is a pretty daunting task (it involves CGI) but, as always, there's someone out there to do the work for you.

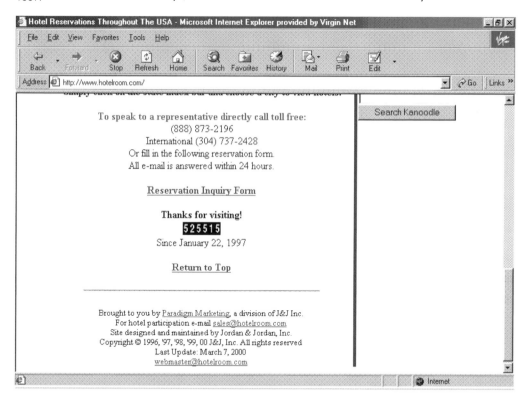

Using your ISP counter

Your ISP will almost certainly provide a CGI program offering a counter that can be displayed in several different styles. To add these counters to your web site is usually straightforward. Your ISP will provide you with the HTML code to do this. The following example illustrates the code provided by Virgin Net:

```
< IMG SRC=http://freespace.virgin.net/cgi-bin/counter.cgi?
uname=brendan.murphy >
```

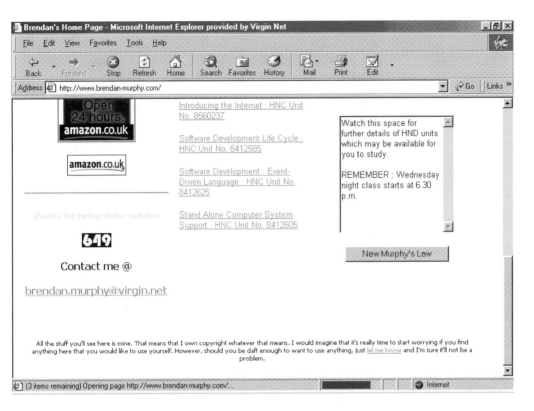

When displayed in a browser window, the above HTML translates to a beautifully displayed counter.

Free counter sites
As always, the wider internet provides resources for adding counters to your page. Pay some of these sites a visit but remember, there's no such thing as a free lunch. If you use any of these counters, it might mean having to carry some automatic advertising from the company concerned.

Sitemeter
http://www.sitemeter.com
Not only can you download free web counters from this site but you are also provided with a wealth of other useful information about your site visitor ratings, such as the number of visitors per hour and per day. You can also register here and receive email details of any further freebies that become available. There are 10 different counter designs to choose from, each having configurable text and background colour schemes.

Counter4Free
http://www.counter4free.com
Visit Counter4Free and choose a counter from over 50 designs. Simply point to a WYSIWYG counter on screen and sign up. Counter4Free has little advertising, so it's a good choice for your web site.

Fig. 69. Example of a home page with a counter (left centre on the page). It is the home page of the author of this book, and displays the fact that there have been 649 visits to his site.

Getting feedback ....

WebSite Design
http://www.websitedesign.com
If you're really sneaky then this is the site for you. With the counters offered you can determine the starting value of the count. This means that instead of your counter showing the number 23 or 110 visitors, you can begin at a much higher value, say 5,000. Of course this is completely misleading in making your site seem much more popular than it really is! With over 10 designs available and an online magazine giving tips to web site designers, this site is certainly worth a visit.

Xoom
http://counter.xoom.com/
This is a very popular site for web site designers. You can register for your free counter, with HTML code details being sent to you by return email. Also, you can sign up for 'Powerstats', a utility which gives you extra details about your visitors such as which sites they are coming from, and what type of browser they are using to access your site. This is a very good site that offers many resources that you could well find useful.

Questions and answers

Do I need to install a special email program to use the 'mailto:' tag for feedback?
No. The 'mailto:' tag will launch the proprietary mail package that you use, and that was provided by your ISP.

Can I write my own HTML visitor counter?
Yes. However, it's quite a difficult task. It's much easier to use the ones provided by your ISP or the free counters offered by the many third party companies found on the world wide web.

Case studies

Doreen likes to hear from guests
Doreen runs a successful bed and breakfast establishment in the English Lake District. For the past five years she has kept a visitor's book in reception, so that guests can record comments about their stay. Doreen has now replicated this book on the B&B web site. Guests with internet access at home can leave comments or request information from Doreen online.

Maxine's friends visit
Maxine's school friends tell her that they love her web site, which is dedicated to modern music. To count the number of visitors to her site – and to feed her teenage ego – Maxine has decided to install a visitor counter on her site. Her ISP provides her with an easy-to-use counter and the HTML code needed to install it easily.

8 Linking with the outside world

In this chapter we will explore:

▶ *creating links to other world wide web pages*

▶ *creating internal links within an HTML document*

▶ *using an image as a link*

· ·

Creating links to other world wide web pages

When you complete the design of your web site it will probably consist of several HTML documents, or web pages. This in itself shouldn't cause you too many problems. However a new visitor to your site may find it difficult to get around. Similarly, your site might contain information where there are lots of resources available elsewhere on the world wide web. In this case you would probably want to provide your visitors with a means of accessing all these resources as well as information on your own web site.

In both cases, the answer is 'hyperlinks'. A hyperlink is simply a piece of text (hypertext) or an image that, when clicked, loads a different page from the current web site, a new web site altogether, or jumps to a new place in the current HTML document.

Hyperlinks offer a quick way of navigating through your web site. By clicking on a word, phrase or image, you can quickly jump to a new source of information.

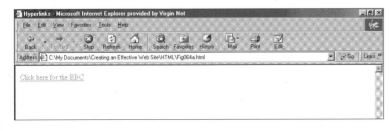

Fig. 70. A web page hyperlink that leads to the BBC web site. If you could click on the link, the BBC web site would be displayed in your browser window.

Linking to another web site

Figure 70 shows the link from one web page to another on the world wide web. The HTML code used to create the link is:

<A HREF='http://www.bbc.co.uk'>Click here for the BBC</A>

The anchor (the first 'A') starts the command. It is followed by the 'HREF' (hypertext reference). This indicates that you are about to load a page from the www. The web site address shown in quotes is the actual web site to be loaded, in this case the home page of the BBC. The text, 'Click here for the BBC' is the hypertext link which, when clicked, will load the BBC site. Hypertext links, when viewed with your browser, usually appear in blue underlined text. The '</A>' (as usual) signifies the end of the command.

Linking with the outside world ....

Creating internal links within an HTML document

Another use of anchors is to allow you to navigate through your current HTML document. To do this involves setting up anchors and 'target' areas within each page. Anchors are little index points which. When clicked, they take you to 'targets', which are typically section headings or sub-headings within the current HTML document. Such use of anchors makes a web site very easy to navigate especially if each HTML document is long and contains a number of separate text sections.

Fig. 71a. Writing some simple HTML to create a web page called 'The Business Traveller' (71b).

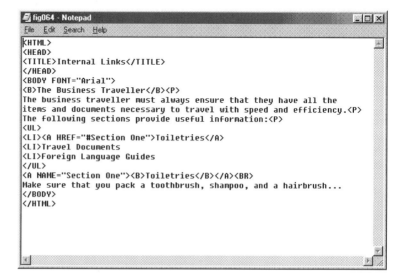

Fig. 71b. Web page generated from HTML in figure 71a.

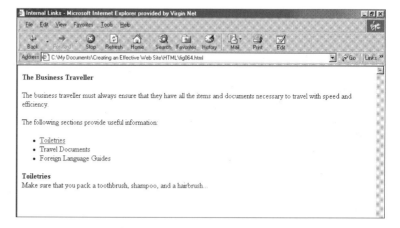

Consider an HTML document that provides checklist information for the business traveller, as in figure 71a. In this example, should your visitors click on 'Section One' in the index, the browser will move them to the part of the document giving the checklist of requirements for business traveller toiletries. The HTML code required to set up this internal link is shown.

In the first hypertext link, instead of pointing to an external www site, the text HREF='#Section One' is included. Use of the '#' sign dictates that the browser should not quit the current document to activate the link. In the second anchor, you create a hidden pointer that says 'when the visitor clicks on '#Section One' then take them to this point in the document.

Using an image as a link

Using images as hyperlinks is a great way to brighten up your web site and make it look very professional. Instead of clicking on a hypertext link, visitors click on a GIF image, causing a different web site to be loaded into their browser. Making an image act as a hyperlink is very like creating a basic hypertext link, explained in the last few pages. The only difference is the insertion of some HTML code that controls the image being 'sneaked' into the anchor tag:

<A HREF=http://www.microsoft.com> <IMG SRC = 'ms.gif' BORDER = 1 > </A>

The 'IMG SRC=filename' allows you to enter the name of the GIF image to be displayed. This image, for simplicity, should be stored in the same area as the HTML document that you are working with. The "BORDER' attribute determines the thickness of the border round the image. (Hyperlinks that are images usually have a border round them to help distinguish them from regular images).

Fig. 72. Writing the HTML to turn the Volkswagen Beetle image into a hyperlink

```
Fig066 - Notepad
File  Edit  Search  Help
<HTML>
<HEAD>
<TITLE>Image Hyperlinks</TITLE>
</HEAD>
<BODY>
<A HREF="www.beetle.fr"><IMG SRC="c:\website\image\beetle.jpg" BORDER=1</A>
</BODY>
</HTML>
```

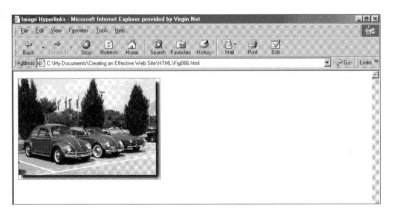

Fig. 73. How the Volkswagen Beetle image would appear on a web page. If you could click on the image (which the HTML in figure 72 has created as a hyperlink), the French web site 'www.beetle.fr' would be displayed in your browser window.

89

Linking with the outside world.....................................

Checklist for creating hyperlinks
1. Always make the hypertext word or phrase obvious to the link being loaded.

2. Keep the image used for links small.

3. Limit your hypertext links to a single word or short phrase.

4. Don't use elaborate images. Instead, use ones that visitors will easily identify with the link being followed.

Questions and answers

What is hypertext?
Hypertext is highlighted text in an HTML document which, when clicked with a mouse, loads a new page in to your browser. Hypertext links can also cause your browser to 'jump' to a new point in your current document.

Can images act as links?
Yes. By adding a simple piece of HTML code to a standard anchor link you can make an image act similarly to a hypertext link.

Case studies

Robert surfs the distilleries
Robert is interested in malt whisky. As part of his hobby, he has created a web site dedicated to the history of a number of his favourite malts. To make the site more useful and interesting, Robert has added hypertext links to the home pages of over 20 distilleries.

Josephine cooks up support on the web
Josephine teaches 'party cooking' at her local community college. To help her students complete their homework and try recipes at home, she has included several images of completed recipes on her site. By clicking on each image, students are directed to the appropriate recipe for the dish on display. Josephine used a digital camera to take the pictures of the food on display.

9 Using frames in your web pages

In this chapter we will explore:

▶ *creating simple frames*

▶ *adding HTML pages to frames*

▶ *forcing frames to load pages where you want them to*

▶ *adding enhanced features to frames*

. . . .

Creating simple frames

Frames are used in HTML documents to enable the browser window to be split into a number of segments. These segments, or 'frames', are usually all horizontal or all vertical with between two and three frames being the norm. Once split, each frame can display an individual HTML document. This gives you great flexibility when designing your site.

Two basic uses of frames are:

1. To create a 'header' frame for your web site which will be displayed no matter where you go on the site.

2. To display an index or table of contents down the left side of the browser window.

Fig. 74. The Glasgow City Council home page illustrates the use of frames. The banner across the top saying 'Glasgow City Council' is a frame. If you click on 'About Glasgow' at the extreme top right, your browser will then display what is shown in figure 75.

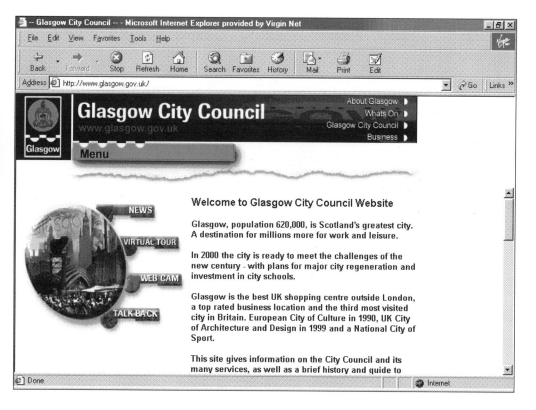

Using frames in your web pages ....

Fig. 75. The Glasgow City Council 'About Glasgow' page. This page has three frames: the banner frame across the top, the navigation frame running down the left-hand side, and the main body frame which mostly fills the browser window.

In the past some browsers didn't like frames causing all sorts of problems when loading HTML documents, however it's fair to say that 99% of browsers now in use will handle frames without too many problems.

Adding HTML pages to frames

Setting up a frames-based home page
Setting up frames within your home page HTML document requires use of two new tags:

<FRAMESET> and <FRAME>

Tag: <FRAMESET>
This tag is used within an HTML document to let the browser know that the page is about to be split into a number of frames. The <FRAME> tag is then used within the <FRAMESET> tag to determine the actual number and style of frames to be used.

<FRAMESET ROWS=30%, 70%>
<FRAME>
<FRAME>
</FRAMESET>

You will notice in the above HTML code, the <FRAME> tag doesn't have a corresponding </FRAME> tag to end the command. Don't worry about this, each <FRAME> tag simply represent another frame on the page. The use of the attribute 'ROWS=30%, 70%' has the effect of splitting your document into two frames, with a horizontal line splitting the browser window 30% from the top.

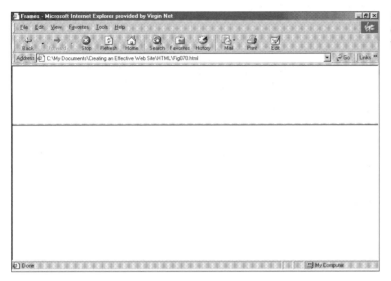

Fig. 76. The basic structure of a web page based on two horizontal frames.

The following HTML code has a similar effect to the code shown above, the main difference being that it splits the screen vertically with a line running top to bottom in the browser window, 15% in from the left side.

```
< FRAMESET COLS=15%, 85%>
< FRAME >
< FRAME >
</FRAMESET>
```

Fig. 77. The basic structure of a web page based on two vertical frames.

Using frames in your web pages ....

Filling up those frames

So, what did you create in the last section? Well, not a lot really. OK, you added some fancy new tags and created some rather stylish, or not so stylish, lines on a page. But what about real contents things that you can look at and click? The < FRAME > tag can now really come in to its own. If you expand the tag slightly and add the attribute 'SRC=filename.html', you can fill your frame up with an existing HTML document. Figures 78 and 79 show this concept in action. You'll notice that the first document loaded is 'frindex.html'. Browsers always fill frames from the left when vertical frames are being used, and from the top, when horizontal frames are being used.

Fig. 78. Writing simple HTML to create frames.

```
File   Edit   Search   Help
<HTML>
<HEAD>
<TITLE>Loaded Frames</TITLE>
</HEAD>
<FRAMESET COLS=15%,85%>
<FRAME SRC="c:\website\frindex.html">
<FRAME SRC="c:\website\fradd.html">
</FRAMESET>
</HTML>
```

Fig. 79. Example of frames created in a web page.

Using hyperlinks with frames

In the example given above you are likely to have a document with some hypertext links that load a different HTML document from your site, or some other place on the world wide web. When the user clicks on one of these hypertext links, the page to be loaded will be displayed in a completely new browser window. Your original framed window is kept active in the background. Of course, this really takes the edge off your web site since your main page is obscured from view and can sometimes be difficult to navigate back to. This is where you can exercise a bit of

'HTML bullying!' You can force your browser to load the new page in the right hand frame of the page, thus keeping some continuity with your page index, loaded into the left frame of your home page.

Forcing frames to load pages where you want them to

The following HTML code sets up your site to force pages loaded via hypertext links to appear where you want them.

```
< FRAMESET COL=15%, 85%>
< FRAME SRC='index.html' NAME='Leftframe'>
< FRAME SRC='intro.html' NAME='Rightframe'>
</FRAMESET>
```

In the above, you have now officially named each frame in your page. One is called 'Leftframe' and the other called 'Rightframe.' Now, any hypertext links loaded in either frame can be amended to point to the appropriate target frame. In the above example, if the user clicked on the words 'Learn the Net Home Page' in the left frame, the following hypertext link code would be carried out:

```
<A  HREF=http://www.learnthenet.com  TARGET='RightFrame'>
Learn the Net Home Page</A>
```

The above site would now be loaded for viewing in the right frame in your browser window.

Adding enhanced features to frames

Using enhanced < FRAME> *attributes*
A useful attribute to stop visitors to your web site messing up your nicely laid out frames is the 'NORESIZE' attribute. It's very easy to use and simply requires that you include it in the < FRAME> tag.

```
< FRAME COL=15%,85% NORESIZE>
```

This will stop visitors being able to drag the vertical and horizontal lines that split the browser window.

Another useful attribute is 'SCROLLING'. This determines whether the frame should always show scrollbars (yes), never show them (no), or show them when required (auto – the default value).

```
< FRAME COL=15%,85% NORESIZE SCROLLING=yes>
```

Checklist for using frames
1. Keep them simple. Anything more than three horizontal or vertical frames can make the whole browser window cumbersome and diffi-cult to read.
2. Ensure that any hypertext links or image links are forced to load into the appropriate frame to help keep the integrity of your web site.
3. Don't allow visitors to resize frames – it'll only cause confusion.

Using frames in your web pages ....

Questions and answers

Can I use frames to create a permanent web site heading?
Yes. By creating two frames split horizontally, you can include a fixed header on your web site.

Are there a maximum number of frames that can be displayed?
No. However, more than three frames per page will make the page very difficult to read.

Case studies

Stephen passes on his knowledge
Stephen has a web site explaining the importance of IT to modern business. It includes his MBA essay on IT. As this essay is some 2000 words in length, with six main sub-heading areas, Stephen wants to make sure his visitors find it easy to read and navigate. By creating a vertical frame of 20%, he has created an index, which links to the main sections in his essay.

Mark resizes his frames
Mark has created a web site for his privately-owned nightclub. Some of his regulars have noticed that they can resize the frames on his home page. Mark has redesigned the site, including the 'NORESIZE' attribute, thus ensuring that visitors cannot amend his frames.

10 Publishing your pages on the internet

In this chapter we will explore:

▶ *publishing your web pages onto the internet*
▶ *using FTP software*
▶ *helping visitors to access your free space*
▶ *registering your own domain name*

In this chapter we'll look at some useful extras to finish off your study of HTML. Now that you've created those all singing, all dancing HTML web pages, you'll likely to want to publish your work on the world wide web. Then, once you are safely installed in cyberspace you'll want to make sure that people can find your web site and access it easily. And finally, just like that private car registration plate, you'll need your own domain name on the world wide web to make it easy for folk to visit, and to give you that memorable personal edge.

Publishing your web pages on the internet

The term used to describe the publishing of your web pages on the world wide web is 'uploading.' Just as you would 'download' a graphic image or piece of software from the world wide web, so you can 'upload' your web pages to the world wide web for all to access.

Your ISP will allocate you some free web space when you join up. This allows you to have a home where you can place your completed web site. Just like your own PC, your ISP has a super-duper PC ('server') which has a permanent connection to the world wide web. This means that, when you transfer your files over to this server, they are available for access 24 hours a day, 365 days a year (barring system crashes).

All ISPs will give you information on how best to upload your files. However, the rules are generally pretty standard. The main software used is an FTP program, of which there are several versions.

Using FTP software

File transfer protocol (FTP) is the method used to send files back and forth across the internet. For example, to transfer your HTML pages from your home PC to your ISP's server requires the use of FTP software. Two very popular software products for doing this are:

WS_FTP (from http://www.ipswitch.com)

CuteFTP (from http://www.globalscape.com)

The basic steps for using each program are outlined below. Both are obtained free from the world wide web. Not surprisingly, they too are downloaded using FTP. Before you try either of these two packages, remember to log on to the world wide web through your ISP. You have to be online to use FTP software for uploading web pages.

Using WS_FTP
1. *Setting up session properties* – When you start WS_FTP you will be presented with the 'Session Properties' window. This allows you to create accounts for all your ISPs, allowing you to transfer files to each ISP's web space areas. The first step is to create a 'New' profile. Give your profile a name that means something to you. For example, if you are loading your web pages onto the Demon network, a good choice of name might be 'Demon Free Space'. In the 'Host Name/Address' field, enter the name of the server where your free space is available. Your ISP will provide you with this information. An example might be 'upload.virgin.net'. The only other fields normally requiring an entry are 'User ID' and 'Password'. These will be the same as the ones you use to connect to your ISP. When you've completed the above fields click 'OK'.

Fig. 80. Using WS.FTP is very easy. In the opening 'Session properties' window, you create a profile name of your choice, type in the web address where you will be sending your web pages, leave 'automatic detect' as it is, enter your User ID and password, and click OK.

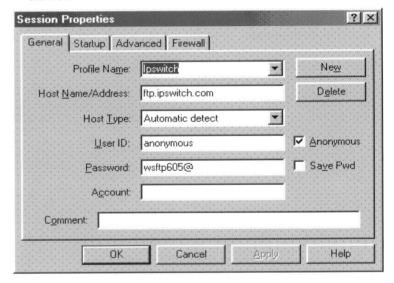

Note – If you've forgotten your username or password call your ISP's helpline. Remember, these calls are likely to be charged at a premium rate.

2. *Transferring files* – Now that you've established a connection with the server waiting to receive your files, WS_FTP presents you with the screen shown in figure 81. In the left pane, your local PC directory structure is shown. On the right, you can see your private free space area on your ISP's server. You can now use the 'ChgDir' or navigational icons in the left pane to find the area on your PC where your web pages are stored. When you've found them, just click on the HTML, GIF and JPEG files you want to be copied. Then click the right arrow button in the centre of the screen to transfer your files. The transfer of each file only takes a few seconds. And that's it, you've successfully transferred your HTML pages onto the world wide web.

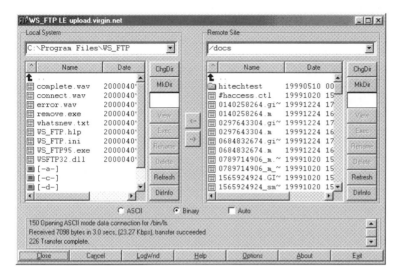

Fig. 81. The WS_FTP transfer screen. The left-hand pane displays the files on your computer, and the right-hand pane displays the files in your web space on the internet. Highlight any file on the left, click the arrow between the panes, and the file will be copied into the right-hand pane.

Using CuteFTP
CuteFTP is fast, friendly and simple. The simplicity of CuteFTP probably comes from its use of 'wizards' that guide you through setting up your connection.

1. *Completing the Connection Wizard screens* – When you load CuteFTP you will be presented with the 'connection wizard'. This will guide the setup of your connection to your ISP. Simply follow through the screens completing your ISP name, a label to help you remember this connection (just like in WS_FTP), your FTP host name, user ID and password, and the default local directory on your own PC where your HTML files are waiting to be loaded.

Fig. 82. The Cute FTP wizard screen. There is a Help button, in case you are not sure what to do next.

99

Publishing your pages on the internet...............................

2. *Transferring files* – In CuteFTP, uploading files to the world wide web is a breeze. Firstly, highlight in the right pane of the 'Site Manager' screen the connection that you've just created. Then click on the 'connect' button. In a few seconds you'll be connected to your free web space area on your ISP's server. To upload files to the web simply drag each file from the left window (your PC) to the right window (your ISP free space area).

Fig. 83. The Cute FTP site manager. The layout is quite similar to WS_FTP (figure 81): there is a pane on the left showing your own computer files, and a pane on the left representing the web space you are sending them to. Here, just one file has been sent, 'cc01.html'.

Uploading all files
Remember, although your main activity has been creating HTML pages, these pages will also include various GIF and JPEG images. Make sure that these image files, too, are uploaded onto your free web space area. Otherwise when your pages are loaded into a browser a horrible little space will appear where your graphic images should be loaded.

Helping visitors to access your free space

Now that you've successfully uploaded your web site onto the web, you'll want to let your visitors know which address to type in to their browser to access it. Your ISP will give you this information. For example:

With FreeServe you type: http://www.yourname.freeserve.co.uk
With Virgin Net you type: http://vzone.virgin.net/yourname/

Defaulting to your home page
When your visitors access your web site you have two methods of loading your home page. The first, and most straightforward, is to call the main page of your site 'index.htm' or 'index.html'. Most browsers automatically look for these file names and load them when visitors enter a site. (Don't worry if your main page is called something else; use Windows Explorer to rename it.)
 The other method is to maintain the name that you chose at the start of

your development and simply ensure that visitors use this at the end of the address. For example if your home page was known as 'mpage.htm' and Freeserve was your ISP you could direct visitors to:

http://www.yourname.freeserve.co.uk/mpage.htm

Registering your own domain name

In the above examples, the address of your home page is rather long and difficult to remember. Many organisations now offer the opportunity to purchase domain names that are easier for visitors to remember. (The author's domain name is 'www.brendan-murphy.com'.) Now, for very little money, you can have a more meaningful name that is much easier to use. Domain name registration is carried out by accessing one of the many companies available on the world wide web. Have a look at the following site, which provides a simple and inexpensive way to search for and register your domain name:

http://www.uk2.net

Finding your web site
If your visitors are personally known to you, or if you've promoted your web address very heavily, then you should have no problem attracting visitors. However, for most private individuals and organisations, the main method they will use to find your site is to look up your name via a search engine, such as Yahoo!, Altavista, Lycos, Excite or Infoseek. This method is also an excellent opportunity to pick up business or interest, since search engine users hail from all four corners of the earth. HTML provides you with a great little tag known as <META>. This can help ensure that you are easily found on the web.

Tag: <META>
The <META> tag has many uses, but you will mainly use it to help publicise your web site. By placing this tag between the </TITLE> and </HEAD> tags you can ensure that search engines find your pages when users carry out a search. The <META> tag goes something like this:

<META DESCRIPTION='The web site of Jim Hughes' NAME=
'keywords' content='football, history, south-indian cooking'>

In the above HTML code, the DESCRIPTION attribute is where you store the words that the search engine will return as the name of your site. The CONTENT attribute shows words that can be searched, each separated by a comma.

11 Using Microsoft FrontPage Express

In this chapter we will explore:

▶ *starting with FrontPage Express*

▶ *creating a basic web page*

▶ *formatting your web page*

▶ *adding some professional touches*

▶ *adding an image to your web page*

▶ *creating hyperlinks*

▶ *creating a feedback form*

. . . .

Starting with FrontPage Express

FrontPage Express is the entry level web design package from Microsoft. Essentially, it is a cut-down version of the popular commercial packages Frontpage 98 and FrontPage 2000. Though it contains less functionality than these, it has lots of useful tools to help you create simple but attractive web pages.

The chief benefit of FrontPage Express is that it's very like Microsoft Word. All the formatting commands are the same, and it has the same look and feel of Word. It provides a WYSIWYG user interface ('what you see is what you get'). This means that the web pages you create using FrontPage Express will look the same – most of the time – when viewed using popular browsers such as Internet Explorer and Netscape Navigator.

Loading FrontPage Express
To load FrontPage Express from your PC, choose Start, then Programs. FrontPage Express may be in one of various folders, but here (figure 84) it is in Accessories, then Internet Tools.

Fig. 84. Opening FrontPage Express from your PC's desktop. Click, Start, then Programs, and locate FrontPage Express. In the computer illustrated here, it is in the Accessories folder, in a subfolder called Internet Tools.

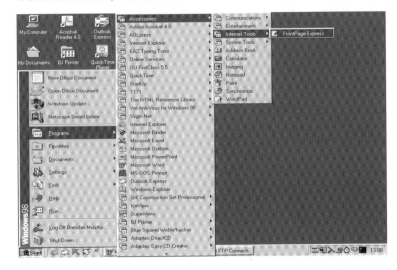

Fig. 85. A FrontPage Express new blank page. Start typing some text!

Creating a basic web page

Once loaded, you are presented with a blank screen as illustrated in figure 85. You could start and type up your first web page here, however it's best to start by actually using the File menu to create a new page. From this menu choose New. You now have a number of choices to make as to the type of page to be created. Keep it simple, and choose Normal Page. You can now get typing and create your first web page. Figure 87 shows a typical first web page.

Whilst this web page is functional, in that it provides some information, it really isn't very pleasing to the eye. In a moment, we'll add some basic formatting, but first you need to save your file on your PC. When you do this you'll notice that a double space is placed between each list entry. This is because a carriage return is the same as placing a <P> tag in HTML. It throws a blank line. If you want your list to appear without the extra line between entries,

Fig. 86. Choosing a new page in FrontPage Express. Six basic templates are offered to get you started. A 'Normal Page' (highlighted) means a basic blank web page, ready for you to add your own text, headings and layout.

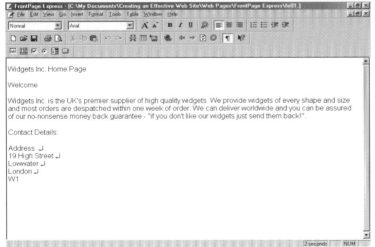

Fig. 87. Starting a FrontPage basic web page, for a hypothetical company called Widgets Inc.

Fig. 88. Storing your web pages and images in Windows Explorer. Here, for example, they are stored in the main folder called My Documents. Into this a sub-folder has been inserted, called Creating an Effective Web Site, and within that another one called 'Html' (highlighted).

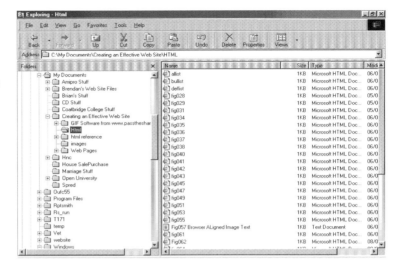

hold down the shift key before pressing carriage return. This is known as a 'soft carriage return'. It has a similar effect as the < BR > tag used in HTML.

Saving your web pages

The best place to save your web pages is in one particular area, or folder, on your PC. For example, you could create a folder for this purpose, and name it something like 'My web pages'. You will then find it easy to upload your pages and any image files to the world wide web once you have completed your design. The best way is to use Windows Explorer to create a suitable folder structure. Figure 88 shows a typical set up. Once completed, you will be ready to save some files into the newly created folder.

Fig. 89. A FrontPage formatted web page, for the hypothetical company, Widgets Inc.

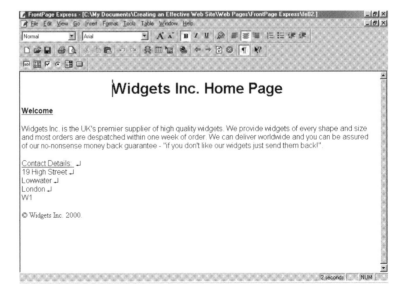

Formatting your web page

Look at the revised version of the sample web page in figure 89. Notice the differences? By adding some of the simple techniques familiar in any word processing package. The page is already looking a lot more professional.

Using bold, underline and italic
To make text **bold**, simply highlight the required text by dragging it with the left mouse button remaining depressed and then simply click the bold icon on the toolbar. The highlighted text should now be displayed in bold. To remove bold, simply highlight the text and once again click on the bold icon on the toolbar. To use underline and *italic*, use the same method as above using the appropriate icons from the toolbar. To mix and match these effects simply highlight the text once and click on any combination of the formatting icons.

Aligning text
In the example shown, the first line of text on the page is centred. Any text can be aligned on a web page in either left alignment, centred, right-aligned or justified. Probably the most effective is left alignment; this will show ragged edges in the right margin. Right-aligned text will show ragged edges in the left margin, centred will centre all text in the centre of the browser window, whilst justified will give a blocked, symmetrical and rather formal effect. Choose the appropriate alignment from the toolbar icons.

Changing the font and font size
Your computer will have several fonts (typefaces), probably including Arial and Times New Roman. You may have many others. To change either the font itself, or the font size, is very straightforward. You can alter the complete text size, and typeface, by choosing the Edit, Select All option from the Edit menu. Or, you can left-click and drag to highlight all elements of the page. Once you've done this, just right-click and change Font Properties. You can also change the font style by highlighting text and using the drop down boxes on the toolbar.

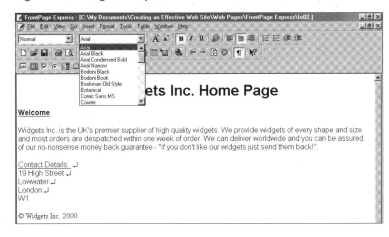

Fig. 90. The FrontPage toolbar, showing the drop-down menu for fonts. Here, Arial has been selected for the main heading 'Widgets Inc. Home Page'. You can see from two highlighted square buttons on the toolbar that the author has selected bold type and centred alignment for the heading.

Using Microsoft FrontPage Express ....

Using pre-defined text types

If you look at the left-hand drop down box on the main FrontPage menu you'll see that it consists of a list of text types (figure 91). These can be quickly used to change the look of a portion of highlighted text. Try highlighting a piece of text and apply some of the styles listed. In particular, the 'heading' styles are useful for web designers. They can be effectively used to ensure uniformity in the treatment of headings and sub-headings used on web pages.

Fig. 91. Another drop-down menu in FrontPage allows you to format headings in different sizes, as here (Heading 3, highlighted).

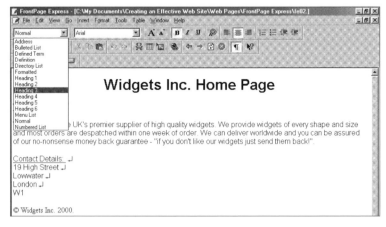

Adding background colour

Now that you've created some text effects, you might want to brighten up the background of your web page. You can either change the background colour, add a tiled (automatically repeated) image, or incorporate both these effects. Try right-clicking anywhere on your page and choosing Page Properties (figure 92). Alternatively, choose Page Properties from the File menu. Now click on the background tab and open the list of available colours on the Background field.

You can now simply choose an appropriate colour for your background or point to a suitable image to be displayed on the background or both. Remember that changing your background colour could affect

Fig. 92. You can specify some general properties for your web page, in FrontPage Page Properties. For example, you can select background colours (or a background image), margins, and other variables.

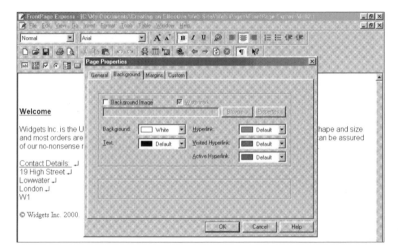

106

the ease of reading of your web page text. Take a moment to change the colour for this field also. A useful hint for beginners is to keep it simple and subtle – black text on a very light eggshell background works very well. Should you wish to create a unique colour then choose 'Custom' and mix and match to suit your own tastes.

Using default colours
You'll probably find that you settle on a background colour for your web site that you want to be reflected through all pages. Choose this colour from the Text Colour icon on the toolbar and add it to your custom colours (figure 93). This colour will now be available for use throughout your web site.

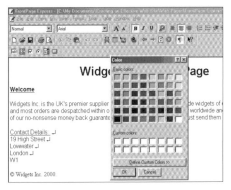

Fig. 93. The FrontPage colour palette is easy to use. Just click on the colour(s) you want for your page background. It's best to avoid very dark background colours.

Adding some professional touches

When visitors arrive at your site you want it to look as professional as possible. FrontPage lets you add nice touches such as a page title. This title will be displayed at the very top of the browser window in the Title Bar. Also, you can add a copyright symbol to show that the web site and its contents legally belong to you.

Adding a page title
Either right-click from your web page and choose Page Properties, or choose Page Properties from the File menu. In the General tab, change the title of your page to suit your own requirements (figure 94).

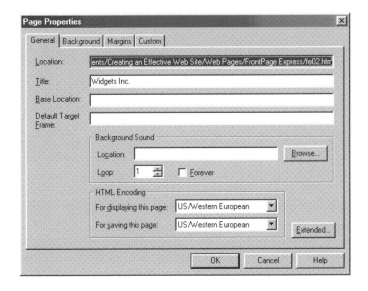

Fig. 94. FrontPage Page Properties, the 'General' tab. Here, you can give a title to the page your are working on (in this case 'Widgets Inc'). You can even add a background sound by selecting a sound file on your computer.

Adding a copyright symbol

To add a copyright symbol to your web page, simply place the cursor at an appropriate point in the text. Then, from the Insert menu, choose Symbol. You will now have an array of symbols to choose from. Choose the copyright symbol, or any other symbol you want, and click Insert and then Close. The symbol will now appear in your web page. Add any appropriate text after the symbol.

Fig. 95. A FrontPage web page incorporating a special symbol, in this case the well-known copyright symbol .

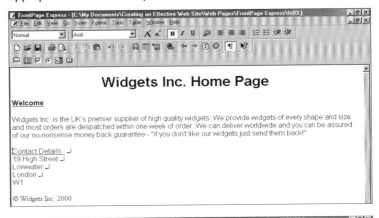

Fig. 96. The Widgets web page has now had a list added to it (services, retail price list and delivery details).

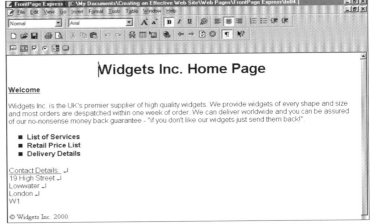

Adding bulleted and numbered lists

Bulleted and numbered lists ensure that your visitors' eyes are drawn to the main points on your web site. It's very easy to create a bulleted or numbered list in FrontPage Express:

1. The first involves positioning the cursor at the start of the line where you want the list to begin. Then, either choose the numbered list or bulleted list icon from the toolbar, or choose the menu option Format, Bullets and Numbering. Now, choose the style of bullets or numbers you want. Then type your list, adding a carriage return after each entry.

2. The second method simply involves highlighting your list and then using the numbered list or bulleted list icon from the toolbar. To remove bulleted or number lists, just highlight them and choose the 'Reduce Indent' icon from the toolbar.

Adding an image to your web page

What's a web page nowadays without some graphic images? Using FrontPage Express you will find it very easy to add GIF or JPEG files to your web pages. To add an image:

1. Place your cursor on the page position where you want the image to appear.

2. Choose the Insert Image icon from the toolbar (or the Insert Image menu command) to begin adding your image. Make sure that the From File radio button is highlighted, and browse and load your image from your PC.

The chances are that the loaded image will look a bit strange. It'll either be far too big or far too small for the page, or the text around the image will look out of alignment. To resize the image, simply click on it to highlight it and use the handles to drag your image to the desired size. You'll notice that the image maintains its proportion when being resized.

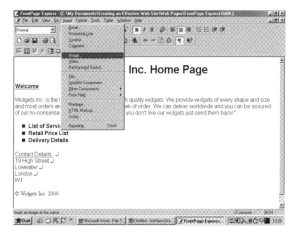

Fig. 97. The FrontPage image menu. By clicking Insert, then Image (highlighted here), you can browse (look through) the files on your computer to select the image file you want to insert into the page.

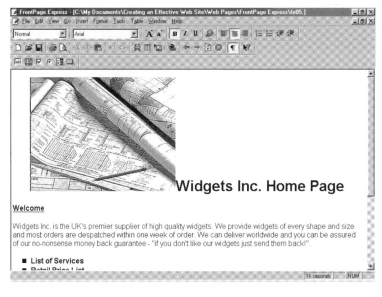

Fig. 98. The Widgets web page has now had an image added to it.

Using Microsoft FrontPage Express ....

Fig. 99. A FrontPage web page with a resized image (compared the size with the image in figure 98).

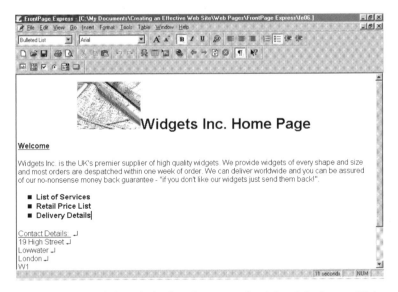

Now all that's left to do is align the text to the right of the image. Right click on your image and choose Image Format from the quick menu displayed. Choose the Appearance tab and in the Alignment field select a few choices until your happy with your image.

Adding a hyperlink

Hyperlinks allow you to quickly load other web pages or areas within your current web page. They work by letting visitors to your site click on a

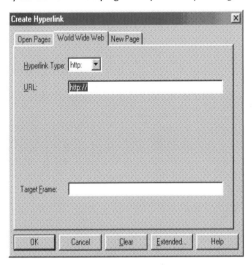

Fig. 100. Creating a hyperlink in FrontPage. Just type in the web address you want to link to for example http://www.bbc.co.uk and click OK. The link on your web page to the BBC will then be working. It's as simple as that.

text link which describes the page being loaded. For example, Widgets Inc. could have a hyperlink from their list of services to another page on their site listing their actual services. All you have to do is highlight the text you want to load the new page. Then, from the Insert Menu choose Hyperlink. In the URL field enter the path of the HTML document to be loaded (figure 100).

Following a hyperlink
Before you upload the pages that make up your web site onto the web, you want to make sure that everything works as it should especially the hyperlinks. To do this, choose the Follow Hyperlink command from the Tools menu. You can also use the Forward and Back commands here to

110

Fig. 101. An example of a FrontPage hyperlink. Notice that 'List of services' is now underlined, telling us that it is a hyperlink. The link leads to another web page within the same web site, containing details of the company's services.

traverse through the pages you've just opened.

Note: You may follow the hyperlink of a link that loads an external web site, say http://www.disney.com. You then get an error message telling you that the file can't be opened. Don't worry. Provided that the web page address is spelt correctly the file will open when accessed online.

Removing a hyperlink

To remove a hyperlink, first highlight the hypertext link, then choose Clear from the Insert Hyperlink menu command on the Insert menu.

Creating an email link

Hyperlinks can also be used to allow visitors to your web pages to easily send you emails. You set up a hyperlink that includes the HTML 'mailto' tag. By clicking your hyperlink, visitors will see a new email message form, with your address details automatically included as the message

Fig. 102. A FrontPage email web page. Notice that 'Contact Details' is now followed by 'email us here' which is an email hyperlink. When someone clicks on it on the internet, it will display an email form containing Widget's email address. The viewer can then easily send an email message to the company.

Using Microsoft FrontPage Express ....

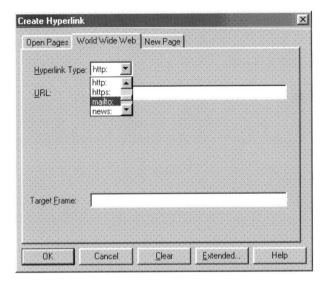

Fig. 103. The FrontPage box 'Create Hyperlink' can be used to create a 'mailto' link. Just type in the email address you want them to reply to, such as 'johnsmith@widgets.co.uk'.

recipient. See figures 102 and 103. To create this type of hyperlink:

1. Choose Insert Hyperlink from the Insert menu.
2. Change the Hyperlink Type to 'mailto'.
3. Enter your email address in the URL field.

Creating a feedback form

Whilst many ISPs will offer statistics about visitors to your web site, these tend to be very basic and lacking in detail. It's much better to offer your visitors a structured form where they can leave information for you to use as a basis for a reply, or to provide more information to them. FrontPage Express allows you to easily create a visitor form for your web site.

To create a form, choose New from the File menu and then Form Page

Fig. 104. Setting up a forms web page using FrontPage Express,

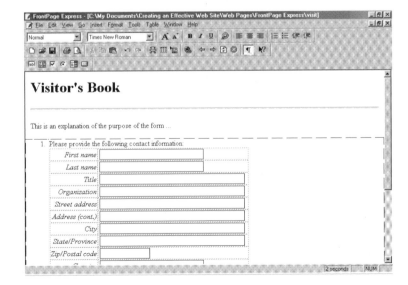

Wizard from the list provided. You will now be guided through the steps required to create a new form. Everything is presented in easy to use, logical steps. You choose a new filename and page title for your form, add specific questions (provided in logical sets such as 'contact information'), decide how the questions on the form should be asked, and decide how the information gathered should be returned to you. See figure 104.

You may want to have your form detail returned to you via a CGI script. In this case ask your ISP for a script that will return form results to your email address. However, this means that you might need to get under the HTML bonnet. With FrontPage Express this is easy. From the View menu, choose to view HTML Source Code. You can now make changes to the HTML code which FrontPage Express has built behind the scenes. (See Part Two of this book for more on HTML.)

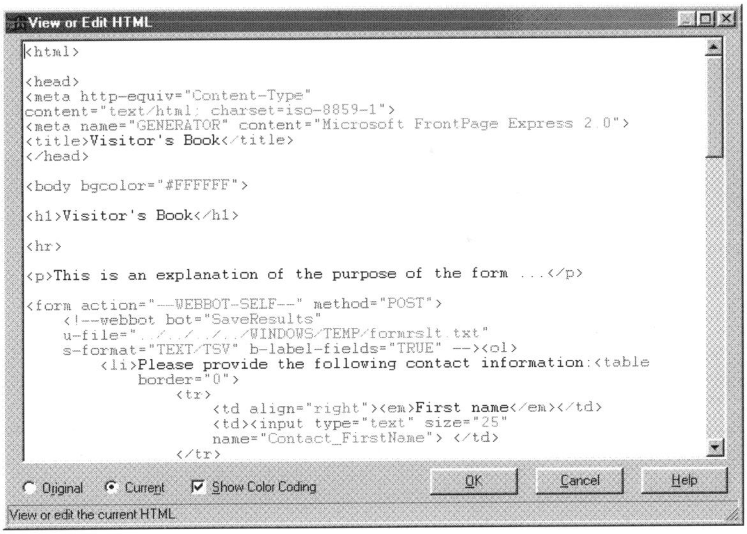

Fig. 105. What a forms web page looks like in the FrontPage HTML view.

Summary

Microsoft FrontPage Express is quick and easy to use. It has a friendly 'front end' that provides a WYSIWYG view, making it easier for beginners to get results fast. It's free and support is provided online from the Microsoft web site.

FrontPage Express is excellent for creating forms, adding tables and defining hyperlinks. It is equally easy to add images and lists and you can create all sorts of wonderful marquee effects. However, online help is poor and, if you choose to view the generated HTML code, it can look a bit daunting. All in all, it's a very basic web editor that is good for beginners but falls short of the functionality offered by its commercial big brothers FrontPage98 and FrontPage 2000.

12 Using Coffee Cup HTML Editor

In this chapter we will explore:

▶ *starting with Coffee Cup*

▶ *creating a basic web page*

▶ *formatting your web page*

▶ *working with tables*

▶ *adding an image to your web page*

▶ *creating and using hyperlinks*

▶ *creating a feedback form*

Starting with Coffee Cup

Introducing Coffee Cup HTML editor
Coffee Cup HTML Editor is a fully-fledged HTML web design package. With over 30 background images, 175 animated GIFs, 140 web icons and other graphics, it is packed with web design tools. It has many excellent features, including a quick-start module designed to get you creating web pages with the minimum of fuss. You can preview your created pages either from within the package or by using your favourite browser. Coffee Cup comes with 24-hour support offered to those registering this share-ware package at a cost of around £18. It can be purchased from: http://www.coffeecup.com

Loading Coffee Cup HTML Editor
To load Coffee Cup, choose Start, Programs, Coffee Cup Software, then Coffee Cup HTML Editor.

Creating a basic web page

Before starting to use Coffee Cup it's a good plan to set some program defaults.

1. From the Tools, Preferences menu, choose the Directories tab.

2. Change the Default Working Directory to a directory that you have set up on your PC to store your web site. It's best to keep all your HTML pages in this one area. It will make it easier to upload them to the world wide web.

3. Choose the Testing & Uploading tab. Change the Favourite Browser field to point to the executable file for the browser you use on your PC. You'll then be able to preview web pages, and see how your visitors will view them when your site goes live.

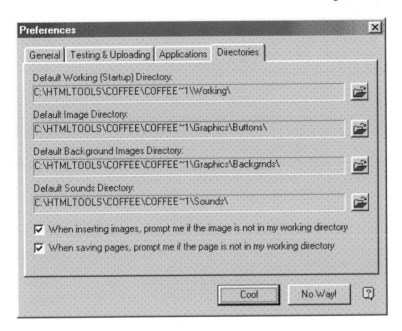

Fig. 106. Coffee Cup Tools, Preferences.

Creating a new page

From the File menu choose New, or New Blank Page. Choosing New allows you to create a basic page, or to select the Quick Start Wizard (this will guide you through the basics - colours of text, page background, hyperlinks, and visited hyperlinks). You can also choose a suitable page title. The benefit is that you get a preview of how the final colour scheme will look, giving you the chance to alter any psychedelic combinations!

Once you've done this, you are presented with the screen shown in figure 107. Coffee Cup is a great HTML editor, though it looks off-putting if your knowledge of HTML is limited. The main web design screen is effectively the HTML code, which normally sits in the background.

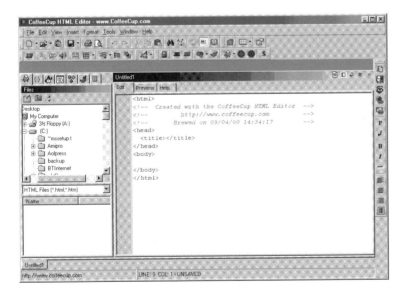

Fig. 107. The Coffee Cup main HTML editing screen. You can see your own computer files in the left-hand pane, while working on a new page in the right-hand pane.

From the main screen, the left window offers seven tabs. These are: Files, HTML Tags, Java Scripts, Dynamic HTML, CGI Scripts, HotStuff, and Snippets. While learning the package, keep the HTML Tags tab highlighted whilst you work.

▶ *Example* – Figure 108 shows a preview of a basic home page for a golf club. The text was entered between the < BODY > and < /BODY > HTML tags. If you just started to type this text you would notice that the text would not, as you type, wrap to the next line in the design window. This won't affect the completed site (remember HTML), but it can make it difficult to work with. To the right of the design window choose the WordWrap icon. This will ensure that you see all the text as you type.

Like Microsoft Word and other word processors, Coffee Cup offers an automatic spelling correction facility. It will call your attention to any misspelt words by underlining them as you type.

A very useful feature of Coffee Cup is that you can use it to preview your pages. Just click between HTML and Preview in the tab to the top of the design window. The Help tab is also conveniently placed here. Unfortunately, you can't change the HTML code from the preview tab, making Coffee Cup less easy to use for those who are not very familiar with HTML .

Fig. 108. A Coffee Cup web page taking shape with HTML.

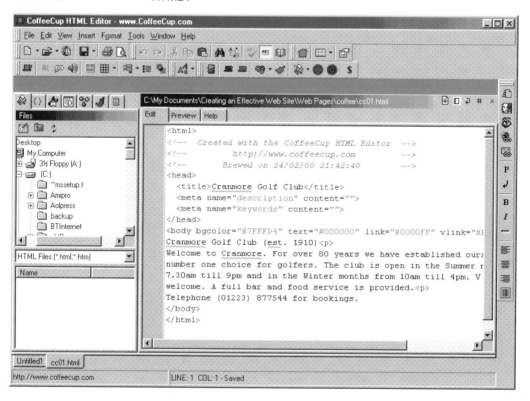

Now that you've created your first web page, it's time to save it and add some formatting. To save your web page, simply choose Save from the File menu.

Formatting your web page

Adding basic formatting
Remember, HTML is all about tags and the text that goes between them. To add enhancements to your web page using Coffee Cup, you'll need to understand how to use HTML tags. For example, to highlight the name of the golf club you need to highlight the heading text with your mouse and then double click on the < B > tag in the left-hand window. This adds the < B > and < /B > tags to the golf club name, to make it display in bold type. This concept is worth mastering early on, as it's used for most activities in Coffee Cup. Help is at hand, however, with the inclusion of an HTML reference guide with the package.

Adding underline and italics works in the same way as adding bold. Just select the text, and double click on both the < I > and < U > tags from the left window.

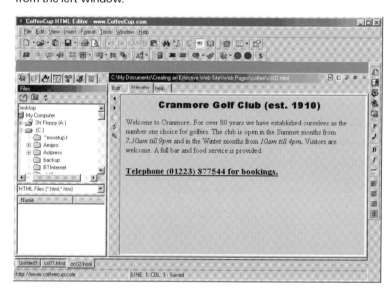

Fig. 109. A formatted web page in Coffee Cup. Note the different text sizes, text alignments, and colour background.

Changing the font and font size
Both the type font used and font size of your text can be easily changed. You can either click on the Fonts icon on the toolbar, or select the Font and FontType menu commands from the Format menu. Here, you can change the Font Size, and Font Colour, and apply several other useful effects.

Using pre-defined font sizes
Using the Header Sizes icon on the toolbar lets you choose from six pre-sized font types. These typefaces can be used for headings and sub-headings throughout your web pages. To use a desired heading size, select the text where the effect is to be applied. Then choose the appropriate heading from the Header Sizes menu.

Using Coffee Cup HTML Editor ....

Changing the colours used on your web pages
In Coffee Cup it isn't that easy to change page colours once you have started. If you're new to HTML the best time to set your colour scheme – the colours for text, background, hyperlinks and visited links – is when you are creating a new page. At this point excellent previews exist to let you see your choices.

If do you want to change colours later, choose the Color Wizard from the toolbar. Next, choose your colour and insert it in the appropriate <BODY> tag. As a guide, the default colours in any HTML document are set in the <BODY> tag:

<BODY BGCOLOR='#ffff00' TEXT='#0000ff' LINK='#0000' VLINK ='#400040'>

To change the above default page colours make sure you insert your cursor in the appropriate area of the <BODY> tag before choosing your new colour from the Colour Wizard icon.

Adding special characters
You can use the View Special Characters icon to insert characters such as currency or copyright signs. Simply place the cursor at the point on your page where the character is to be inserted. Then click the View Special Characters icon, and choose the character to be inserted. It will automatically be placed into that area of the page.

Fig. 110. A Coffee Cup web page with special characters, in this case the copyright symbol .

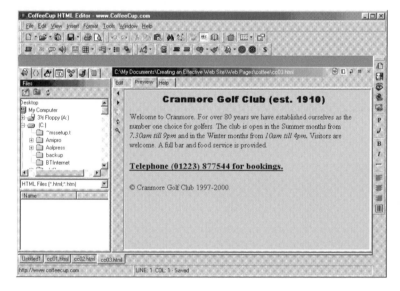

Adding a list
Coffee Cup lets you create all the lists available when you directly create web pages using HTML. Numbered, bulleted and definition lists can all be set up easily. To create a numbered or bulleted list:

1. Click on the Insert List icon on the toolbar, or choose List from the Insert menu (figure 111).

2. From the Insert List dialogue box, simply choose the type and style of the bullets or numbers to be used. Then enter the details of each item of the list being created. You can also insert a list header if you wish.

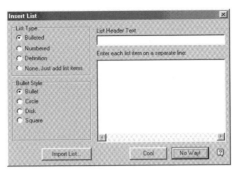

Fig. 111. The Coffee Cup 'Insert List' feature gives you several options for presenting lists, for example numbered, or bulleted in different styles.

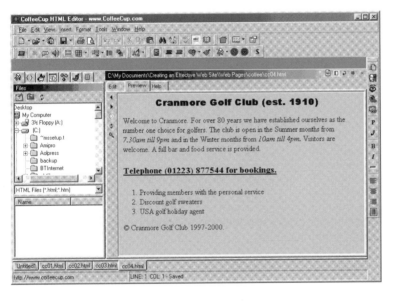

Fig. 112. A Coffee Cup web site incorporating a list (a numbered list of three items).

Removing a list

Unfortunately, the only easy way to remove anything that you've done using Coffee Cup HTML Editor is to get under the bonnet of HTML and hack the code out. This can make things difficult if you are not fully conversant with HTML.

Working with tables

Inserting a table

There are two ways of adding tables to your web pages using Coffee Cup. The first requires a knowledge of HTML, whilst the second is very much automated.

Using Quick Table

By choosing the Quick Table icon from the toolbar you can visually select the number of rows and columns required and drop the table down on to your web page. You will then put your HTML knowledge to the test, and add the contents for your table straight in to the <tr> and <td> tags displayed (figure 113).

Using Coffee Cup HTML Editor ....

Fig. 113. The Coffee Cup
HTML Table View.

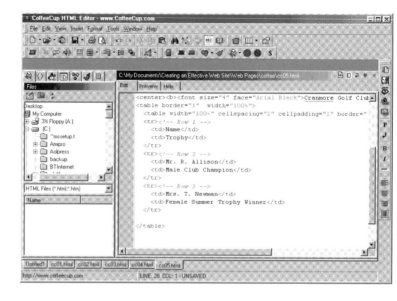

Using menus to add a table

Probably the easiest way to add a table to your web page is to use the
Insert Table icon on the toolbar, or Table from the Insert menu (figure 114).
The dialogue displayed allows you to very easily choose the table rows
and columns, border size, position and colour, as well as actually adding
data easily to your table.

Fig. 114. The Coffee Cup
Insert Table command. You
can easily specify the
number of rows and
headings you want, plus
their dimensions (such as
spacing, padding, width
and height).

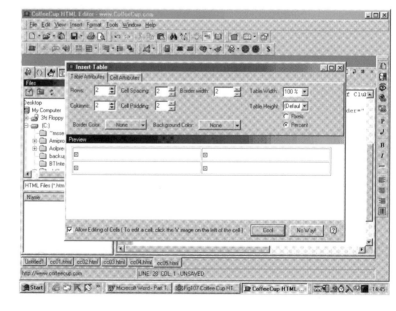

Adding an image to your web page

Inserting an image into a web page is easy. It will help to brighten and add interest to your site. In Coffee Cup choose either the Insert Image icon form the toolbar or, from the Insert menu, choose Image. You will then see a very easy-to-use dialogue box. In the left frame you choose the image from your PC. To the right, you format that image to suit your needs. A preview facility is available. Also, you can make the image a link by simply including the URL of the web page to be loaded by the link.

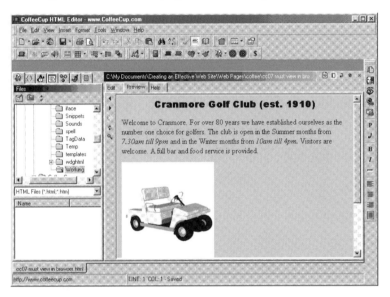

Fig. 115. A Coffee Cup web site incorporating an image.

Using Image Companion
Coffee Cup comes with an extra package called Image Companion. To use this, choose Tools, Image Companion. It is very useful for changing the colours of an image, converting it to greyscale, and rotating it. The contrast, brightness and hue can also be amended here. To change the size of your image it's better to use another popular package such as Microsoft Image Composer, IceView, or GIF Construction Set.

Creating and using hyperlinks

Adding a hyperlink
Once again, adding a hyperlink is very straightforward in Coffee Cup:

1. Simply highlight the text that is to become your link.

2. Choose the Insert Link icon from the right-hand side toolbar.

3. Enter the URL to be loaded when the link is pressed.

You can also add a hyperlink by placing the cursor in the required point in your web page and then choose Insert Link. Enter the text that you wish to be highlighted for your link.

Removing a hyperlink
Like most other things in Coffee Cup, it's time to delve into HTML. To remove a link, highlight the appropriate text (and surrounding HTML code) and delete it from the document.

Adding an email link
Click on the Email Link icon in the toolbar at the right hand side of the screen. Enter the text to be highlighted as the link and then enter your email address in the Email Address link. It's that simple (figures 116 and 117).

Fig. 116. It's easy to insert an email link using Coffee Cup.

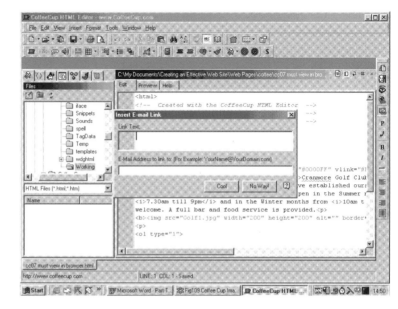

Fig. 117. An example of a Coffee Cup web site with an email link. The email link is to 'info@cranmore.co.uk'.

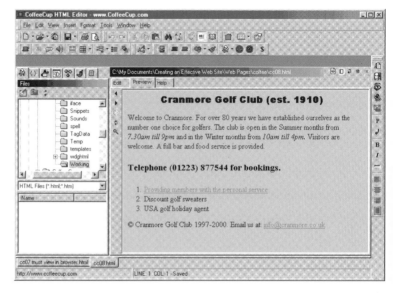

Creating a feedback form

Creating forms using Coffee Cup HTML Editor isn't that easy. It requires some HTML knowledge. Here it is step-by-step:

1. Firstly, create a new page.

2. From the Insert menu, choose Form Items, Insert Form. From here, complete the dialogue box either with CGI information (from your ISP) or with your email address (used for simple form return detail).

3. Build your form by dropping down fields on to it. This is done from the Insert menu. Choose Form Items, and then one of the 14 types available. The most common form fields are Text fields as well as Submit and Reset buttons. (See Part Two of this book for more detail.) Remember to add line breaks (
) after each field that you drop on to your form, otherwise the fields will appear on the same line.

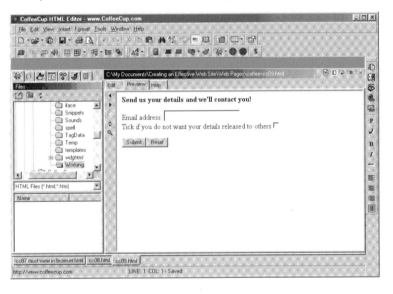

Fig. 118. A Coffee Cup Form web site.

Summary

Coffee Cup HTML Editor is a great product provided you understand HTML. It could be the perfect tool for those who want the speed of a web site design tool with the control and flexibility offered by having a good understanding of HTML. The software is relatively easy to use, and very intuitive. It gives you everything you need to build great web pages, including graphics and java applets. The use of wizards makes things easier, and the ability to preview pages in a live browser is useful.

The extras provided with the package are also good – the Frames Designer and Image Companion in particular. The help screens are thorough, being a mix of explanation and tutorial. Many other help resources are available via Coffee Cup's web site.

All in all this is a very good product, though not suitable for people with a limited understanding of HTML.

13 Using Hotdog Express

In this chapter we will explore:

▶ *introducing HotDog Express*
▶ *creating a basic web page*
▶ *using web blocks*
▶ *managing your new web pages*
▶ *basic formatting*
▶ *adding images to your web page*
▶ *working with hyperlinks*
▶ *adding a horizontal line*
▶ *deleting a web block*

Introducing HotDog Express

HotDog Express is a very easy-to-use web page design tool and is available free of charge on an unlimited trial basis. It allows the easy creation, building and publishing of web pages. It has a very different look to most web design tools, enabling a series of steps from web creation through to publication on the web.

Loading HotDog Express
To load HotDog Express on a PC, choose Start, Programs, Sausage Software, then HotDog Express.

Creating a basic web page

There are two ways to start the design of a new web page:

1. You could choose a pre-defined template. The package only comes with two, and both are fairly basic.

2. You can skip a step and move to 'build your page'. Here, a new web page is automatically created, ready for you to start adding some information.

Creating a page using the templates provided
To choose a template, click on the templates icon in the left pane of the main application window. Make sure the Choose Your Page menu icon is highlighted. Here, you have three choices:

1. blank template

2. Home Page 1

3. Home Page 2

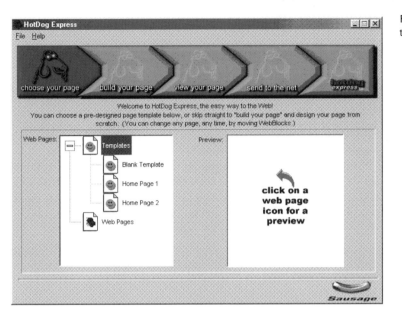

Fig. 119. Choosing a template in HotDog.

To view any of these templates, simply click on the one you want. From the menu icons choose View Your Page. (You can also see a small preview in the right hand pane of the Choose Your Page menu icon.)

Creating a page from scratch
If you don't fancy the rather limited templates provided, you can skip the first stage in the HotDog web design process (Choose Your Page), and jump straight to Build Your Page. Either way, you will end up at the screen shown in figure 120.

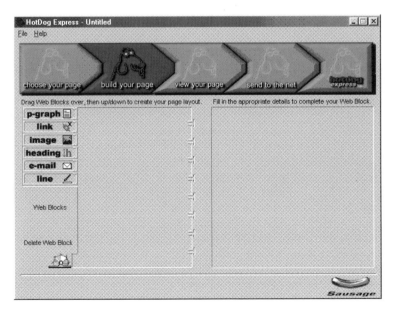

Fig. 120. The 'build your page' screen in HotDog. You drag over 'web blocks' from the left-hand side, then up/down to create the layout and sequence you want.

Using web blocks

At a first glance, the Build Your Page web design screen in Hotdog Express looks rather daunting. Before you go much further, it might be an idea to give yourself a 10-minute run through the software tutorial, which you'll find in the Help menu. This is an excellent source of help, and you will soon see how easy HotDog is to use.

HotDog Express is based on a unique system of 'web blocks' and 'sockets'. To build a page, you click on a block at the left-hand side of the screen, and drag it across to a spare socket at the right-hand side.

You start with the socket at the top of the screen and work your way down. This represents the same order that they will be displayed on your web page. For example, a web page will normally have a heading, some paragraphs of text and some images. A typical HotDog web page might then have the web blocks in sockets as shown in figure 121.

Fig. 121. A typical HotDog screen. Here, four Web Blocks have been dragged across into four sockets. The author is deciding what kind of horizontal line to create.

Web block types
Six types of web block are available in Hotdog Express:

1. *Heading* – This web block enables you to enter heading text for your web page as well as to choose the size and alignment of headings.

2. *P-graph* – This web block is used to enter the text of your web page.

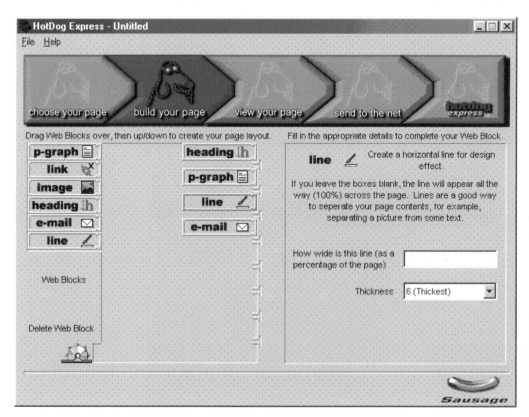

126

3. *Line* – This web block allows you to enter a horizontal line of a desired thickness and percentage size on your web page.

4. *Image* – This one enables you to place a graphic image on your web page. You can choose the image from disk, and adjust its height and width. You can define a text description for those visitors who either cannot - or choose not to - display images in their browser. You can also use this web block to make an image a link allowing you to load another web page by clicking on the image.

5. *Link* – The link web block enables you to enter hypertext links on your web page.

6. *Email* – This web block allows you to set up a standard email hypertext link, called 'mailto:'. This will allow your visitors to easily send you an email via your web page.

You can have as many web blocks of each type as you wish on each of your web pages. As you drag the web blocks into their sockets, they are immediately replenished for re-use.

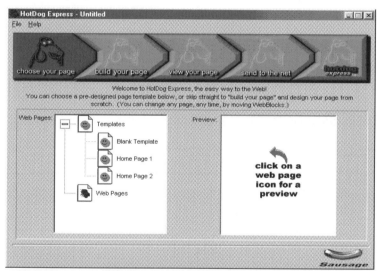

Fig. 122. The HotDog Template Window.

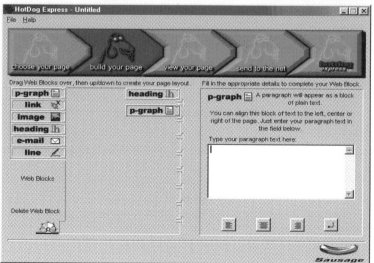

Fig. 123. Two HotDog web blocks in sockets, one for headings and two for paragraph text. The author is working on paragraph text.

Using Hotdog Express...

Fig. 124. The HotDog heading web block. As to the size of heading, the author has specified '3 (large)'. Using the icons at bottom right, he can specify the alignment of the heading.

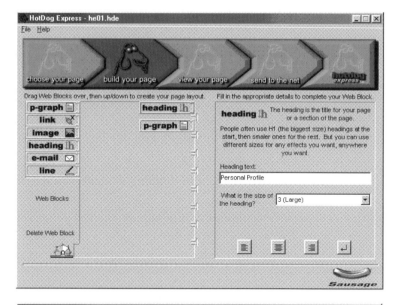

Fig. 125. The HotDog paragraph web block. You enter your text in the white box, and can then align it left, right or centre.

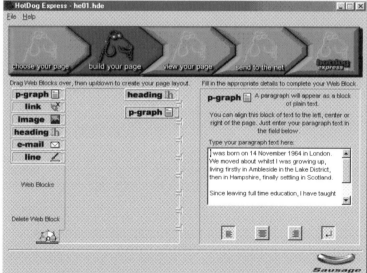

Putting all the web blocks together on your web page

(a) From the main HotDog Express window, double click on the Templates icon. This will display the window shown in figure 122.

(b) Double-click on the Blank Template icon. You will now be automatically guided to build your page. By dragging each web block, copy one heading block and one paragraph block to the sockets to the right of the main window.

(c) Now, click on the Heading web block that you've just added to the top socket. You'll see that you can now add heading details and adjust the size of your heading.

(d) Do the same for the paragraph block, entering some text information.

Managing your new web pages

Saving your web page
Now that you've entered some heading and paragraph detail, it's time to save your web page. From the File menu choose Save. Then save your file in an appropriate folder on your hard disk, such as My Documents, or some other folder you have created for the purpose.

Opening an existing page
To open an existing web page in HotDog Express, choose the Open option from the File menu. Then point to and open your required web page.

Viewing your web page
To view the web page that you've just created, choose the View Your Page menu icon. You can now see how your web page will look when loaded into a browser. Choose the Max icon at the bottom of the screen to see a full-page preview of your web page.

Basic formatting

The unregistered version of HotDog Express comes with few formatting functions. For example, there's no way to make text bold, italic or under-lined.

The only real formatting function available is alignment. Within each web block, alignment icons exist for left, centre and right alignment. By clicking on any of these, the alignment of all the text in that web block will be changed. This means that, if you are looking to introduce a number of different alignment styles in your web page, you would need to split your text into a number of separate web blocks, each with its own alignment type. This is not a problem with HotDog Express, since you are not limited to the number of 'plug and play' web blocks that you can include in your web page.

Changing colours
To preview your page in HotDog Express, choose the View Your Page menu icon. If you look at the resulting options, you'll notice that – at the bottom of the screen – you have the ability to choose a page style (figure 126). There are fourteen styles in all. They give you the option to change the overall text and background look of your web page. Watch your page transformed by simply applying a different style. Try the Weenies, Blue Fade, and Purple Fade styles for some fun and professional designs.

Editing styles
You can edit the styles in HotDog Express to change the text colours, or even create and save your own style. Click on the Edit Style button in the View Your Page section and choose to add, modify or delete a style (figure 127). Then follow the wizard that will guide you through the process of modifying a style. As you change each element a good preview facility is provided, so that you can see if you like it.

Using Hotdog Express..

Fig. 126. The HotDog style views. The style templates on offer (see bottom of screen) include Purple Fade, RoseTiles, Plaster, Tiger Bumps, Sausages, Weenies and various others.

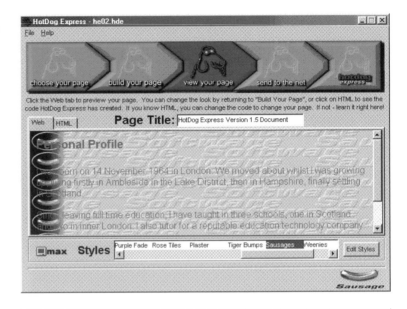

Fig. 127. The HotDog style wizard. You can use it to specify different colours for document text, standard links, active links, and visited links.

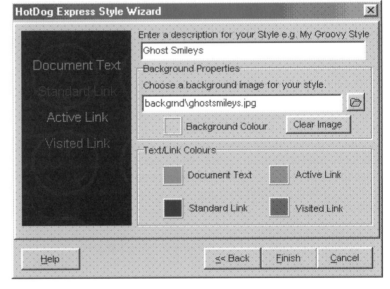

Adding a page title
To add a page title to your web page choose the View Your Page menu icon. Change the Page Title field to the one you want displayed at the top of your visitor's browser window.

Adding images

Adding an image to your web page
To add an image to your web page, go to the Build Your Page menu icon. Grab an image web Block and place it in a socket.

Next, complete the required information. The field 'Enter the location of your image file' lets you choose an image. The Height and Width fields allow you to change the size of the image (remember to keep these values in proportion). The field 'Text description of the image' enables you to enter a textual description of the image. This will be available when visitors 'mouse over' the image when displayed in their browser. Finally, the field 'What is the URL of the page you wish to link to' allows you to name a web page to be loaded when the image is clicked. See figure 128.

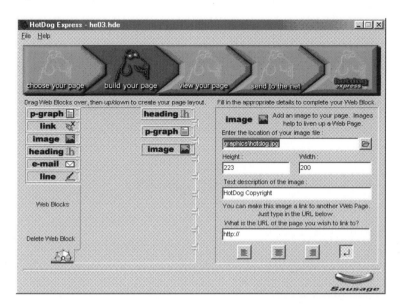

Fig. 128. The HotDog image view. You can use this window not only to add an image to your web, but to convert the image into a hyperlink.

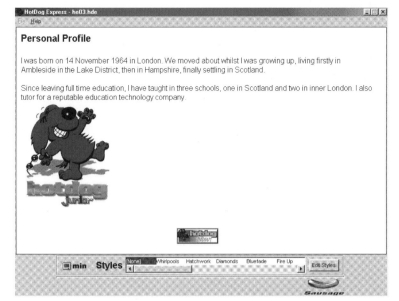

Fig. 129. A HotDog web page. The image and text are displayed in position on the web page.

Working with hyperlinks

Adding a hyperlink

To add a hyperlink to your web page, drag and drop a link web block into the first available socket below the image placed in the previous section. To complete the hyperlink you need to fill out some of the fields on the web block. First, you enter the URL of the page that the hyperlink will load. Then you type in any text you wish to be displayed before the hyperlink. Next you enter the hypertext itself (the text that when pressed will load the required web page). Finally you enter any text that should follow the hyperlink – simple! (figures 130 and 131).

Fig. 130. Creating a hyperlink in HotDog, using a link web block in a socket.

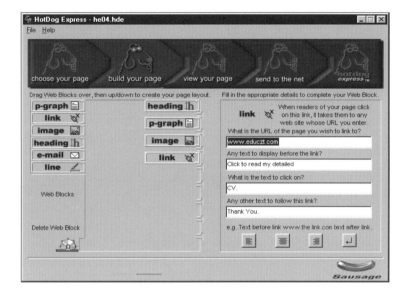

Fig. 131. Viewing a hyperlink on a HotDog web page. The hyperlink is the underlined text 'CV'. When a visitor clicks the link on the internet, it will display a another web page containing CV details.

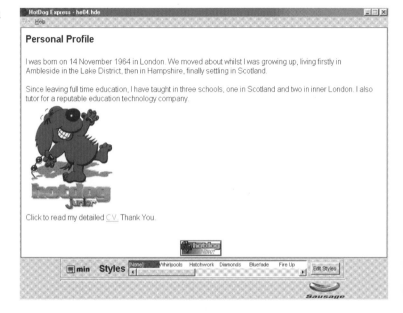

Adding an email link

Adding an email link in HotDog Express is very easy. It follows much the same process as adding a standard hyperlink. The main difference is that, instead of entering the URL of a web page to be loaded should the link be clicked, you enter details of your own email address. When the link is clicked, visitors will be able to very easily send you an email message from your web page (figure 132).

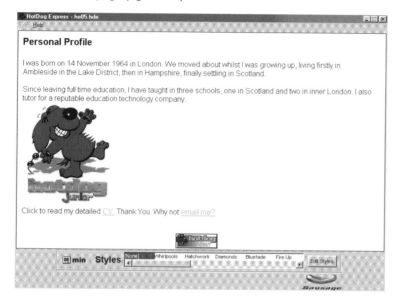

Fig. 132. An underlined email link in a HotDog-generated web page 'Why not email me?' When a visitor clicks the link on the internet, it will display a blank email form containing the web author's address. The visitor can then easily send an email message.

Adding a horizontal line

Adding horizontal lines in your web page means you can split it into sections and make the page easier to read and assimilate. Within HotDog Express, adding a horizontal line is simple. As usual, grab a web block – this time the line web block – and drag it to the next available

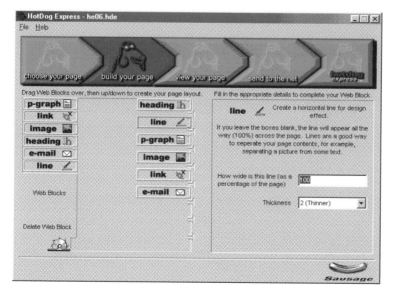

Fig. 133. Adding a horizontal line to a HotDog web page. Adding one or lines will help you to arrange and display your material in a professional-looking way.

socket. In the example shown in figure 133, the line needs to come after the main page heading. To move a web block already in a socket, simply click on it and drag it to the appropriate socket in the web page. When you release your mouse the sockets will move accordingly.

The options available in the line web block are straightforward: choose the desired percentage coverage of the line and its width and there you have it – a perfect horizontal line on your web page (figure 134).

Fig. 134. A finished web page in HotDog, complete with heading, horizontal line, text, image, a CV hyperlink, and email link.

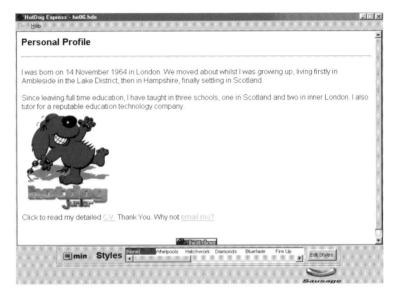

Deleting a web block

HotDog Express has a very innovative method of deleting web blocks. From the BuildYour Page menu icon, just grab the web block in the socket to be removed, and drag it to the 'circular saw' icon at the bottom left of the screen. Watch in amazement as your web block is ripped to shreds to the sound of sawing noises!

Fig. 135. Any unwanted HotDog web blocks can be deleted by dragging them to a circular saw (bottom left), to the accompaniment of a satisfying sound track!

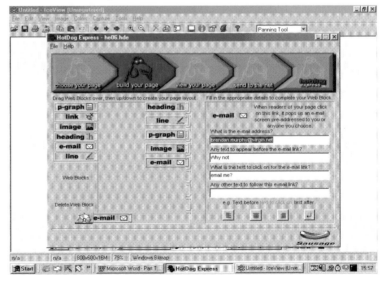

Summary

HotDog Express is an innovative and simple to use web design package. It requires absolutely no knowledge of HTML. It is very visual, and the idea of using web blocks to build pages is well suited to beginners.

However the package is not tremendously functional. For example you cannot make text bold, italic or underlined. Nor can you edit the HTML code behind the pages, though this function is available in the registered copy. Also, if you want to upload your pages on to the web you will need to register the product.

These points aside, it's an attractive package and deserves an 'A+' for innovation and ease of use. A good plan would be to try the package out and then, as quickly as possible, register the package with http://www.sausage.com and begin exploring the full functionality of the registered product.

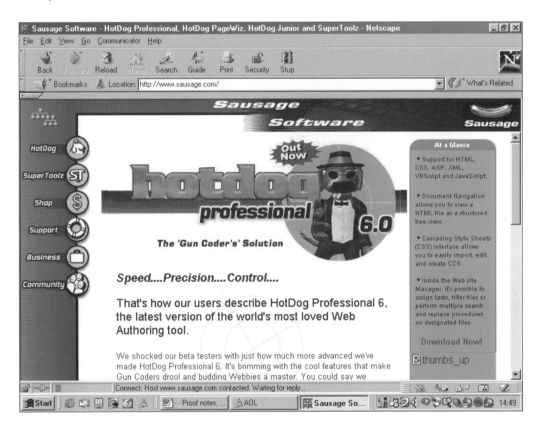

14 Using 1st Page 2000

In this chapter we will explore:

▶ *introducing 1st Page 2000*
▶ *creating a new web page*
▶ *adding basic formatting*
▶ *using other formatting effects*
▶ *checking your spelling*
▶ *adding lists to your web page*
▶ *adding an image to your web page*
▶ *adding an image to your web page*
▶ *working with tables*
▶ *removing formatting, tables, and images*
▶ *adding links to your web page*

. . . .

Introducing 1st Page 2000

1st Page 2000 is a fully fledged HTML web design package. It is available for download and free to use with no registration required. Users are offered three modes: Easy, Expert and Hardcore. Each one allows you to progress through various levels of functionality and complexity depending on your knowledge of HTML. You thus have a route to follow, if you wish, on your journey from beginner to web design expert.

1st Page 2000 also provides support for advanced features such as Java and ActiveX components. Built-in project management for advanced users adds further benefit.

Loading the software
To load the package on your PC, choose Start, Programs, Evrsoft, and 1st Page 2000.

Creating a basic web site
On entering 1st Page 2000, a message reminds you that you are entering 'Easy' mode. It also reminds you that you can switch between Easy and Expert mode whenever you wish while using the application. This will be handy as you become more used to its functions.

The opening screen is the Start Manager (figure 136). This gives you a framework to start building your web pages. The main window gives advice on how to create a new web document and how to use templates. There are some 1st Page 2000 tips and tricks, details of an online HTML reference, as well as details of a more advanced reference guide covering JavaScript and Cascading Style Sheets. To view any of these options just choose the appropriate button to the right of the main window.

Note: Start Manager can be launched at any time by clicking on the Properties icon on the toolbar.

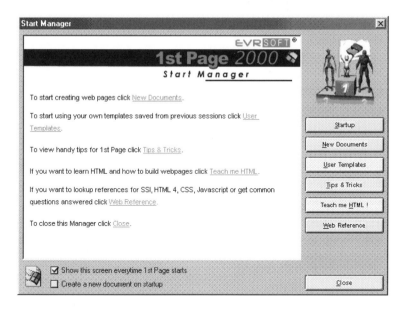

Fig. 136. The 1st Page Start Manager. There are links to start up, templates, new documents, tips and tricks, and some tutorial help with writing HTML.

Creating a new web page

From the Start Manager choose New Documents. You are now presented with a very visual and descriptive list of document types. Choose Blank HTML Document. This will bring up the bare bones of an HTML document ready for you to start building your web page. Now, just add a title for your web page that will be displayed when viewed with a browser. This can be done by adding some text between the < title > and < /title > tags. Continue to enter more text between the < body > and < /body > tags.

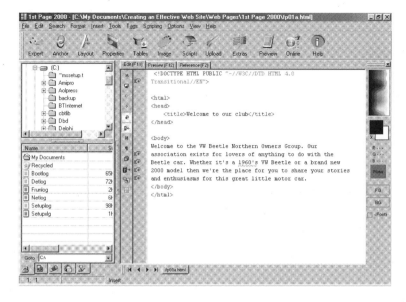

Fig. 137. Creating a basic web site using 1st Page.

Using 1st Page 2000 ....

Fig. 138. What the basic web site in figure 137 looks like when viewed in a browser.

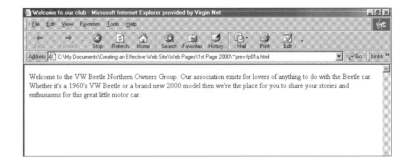

You will notice that, as you type, text that extends beyond the viewing area of the 1st Page window is difficult to read. This can become very distracting. However, the problem is easily solved by turning on the 'word wrap' function. To do this, right-click anywhere in the main window and choose Word Wrap.

Saving your web page
To save your web page choose the Save option from the File menu. Save your web page into an appropriate folder.

Previewing your web page
1st Page 2000 offers a very flexible method of viewing your HTML web pages. You can see a quick preview by clicking on Preview tab at the top of the main window. You can also press the F12 button on your keyboard to get the same preview.
　The package offers a robust method of viewing that will allow you to test your web pages on a number of browsers and browser versions (Internet Explorer, Netscape etc). By clicking on the Preview icon on the toolbar you can define a list of browsers in which to preview your web pages. These browsers must of course be installed on your hard disc. From there they can be accessed and installed in 1st Page 2000 by selecting the AutoSearch button in this menu option. Then, when you click the Preview icon you will have a choice of browsers in which to view your HTML pages.

Opening an existing web page
To open an existing web page, close the Start Manager and choose Open from the File menu. A very useful feature in this menu is the Re-open function. By choosing this option, your most recent web pages are listed giving you quick access to them.

Adding basic formatting

Adding basic formatting effects – such as making text bold, italic and underlined – is straightforward in 1st Page 2000. Highlight the text required. Then right-click with your mouse and choose HTML, Style and then either Bold/Italic or Underline. Other formatting effects such as Strikethrough and Teletype are also available here. From the same menu, this time choose the Size option, and you can then change the size of your highlighted text. A quick way to access many of the effects listed here is through the Layout icon on the toolbar. Again, highlight your text, click on this icon, and choose the effect you want.

Adding a line break
For some reason, HTML doesn't deal very well with line breaks. If you want to take a new line to display a new heading or start a new paragraph, you need to remember to do some DIY! Using 1st Page 2000, place your cursor in your text where you want the line break to come, then choose Line Break from the Tags menu. Or, place your cursor where you want the line break to be inserted, and hold down the Shift-Ctrl-Break keys. (This method should be used if anyone's watching over your shoulder it can make you look very knowledgeable and impressive!) This will have the effect of moving the text following the <BR> tag onto a new line.

   Should you want to do the same thing but leave a blank line before your new text starts, use the Paragraph menu option from the Tags menu. (Sorry, no fancy keystroke options available here!)

Using other formatting effects

Aligning text
To align a segment of text using 1st Page 2000 first highlight the required text. Then right-click, choose HTML, Alignment, Paragraph and choose Left, Center or Right, according to what you want.

Using heading styles
HTML provides six levels of heading size. These are generally used for headings and sub-headings and provide uniformity of design. To create a heading using 1st Page 2000, highlight the text concerned. Then right-click, and choose HTML, and Format. You then choose the heading size you require. Heading 1 is the biggest and Heading 6 is the smallest.

Adding special symbols
Special symbols such as the copyright symbol can be quickly added to your web page using 1st Page 2000. Position your cursor where you want the symbol to appear. Choose the Special Character Symbols option from the Insert menu, choose your symbol, and watch it auto-matically appear in your page.

Changing text and background colours
Changing colours for both the foreground and background text of your web pages is a little tricky with 1st Page 2000.

1. Choose the Document Properties menu option from the Format menu. Here you can choose appropriate colour schemes for your page back-ground and textmatter, as well as for any links, visited links, and active links in your web page.

2. Click on the 'pick a colour' palette icon to choose the colours you want.

3. Your design is previewed as you choose your colour scheme.

Using 1st Page 2000 ....

Fig. 139. The 1st Page HTML color scheme view, where you can specify the text colours.

Once you are happy, click the OK button and your colour scheme is applied. (Check the <BODY> text and you'll be able to see how HTML has assigned the various elements of colour to your web page.)

Checking your spelling

When we type text for our web pages, we are all apt to make spelling mistakes. 1st Page 2000 comes with a useful LiveSpell function. This will check your spelling as you type, underlining in red any apparent mistakes. Choose the LiveSpell option in the Tools menu to toggle this function off or on. If it is switched off, pressing the F7 key will run a spell-check manually. Pressing the Shift-F7 keys will display a useful thesaurus check for words that you might feel need to be replaced. This option can also be found in the Tools menu.

Adding lists to your web page

1st Page 2000 provides access to the standard HTML lists – unordered (bullets), ordered (numbers), and definition. To create a list within your web page, place the cursor at the point in the page where a list should be placed, then (to choose the type of list) right-click and choose HTML, List, and select your required list type (figure 140).

This will have the effect of setting up a blank list ready for you to add your list items. For example, if you had chosen the unordered list, you will probably now see the <UL> </UL> tags being shown where you placed your cursor. Now, all you have to do is enter the contents of your list. To do this, make sure that your cursor is placed between the <UL> and </UL> tags. Now, right-click and choose the HTML, List option, and then choose the List Item option. This has the effect of placing a blank list item between the <UL> and </UL> tags. Now, enter the text of this list item:

<UL> <LI> £17 per annum membership </UL>

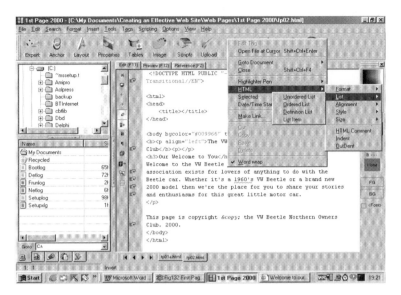

Fig. 140. The 1st Page list view. Using the drop-down menu, you can select different types of lists, such as ordered or unordered.

Repeat the process adding further list items to your list.

Fig. 141. What a 1st Page bulleted list looks like when viewed in a browser.

Adding an image to your web page

Adding an image using 1st Page 2000 is simplicity itself. Simply click on the Image button on the toolbar, then choose the option Insert Image Quickly. Locate and open your image, and it appears just where you want it.

Working with tables

Adding a table to your web page
To add a table to your web page, choose the Tables icon from the toolbar. This will display a dialogue box which, when completed, will draw your table for you. Enter the number of rows and columns you want. Next, click on each cell at the bottom of the dialogue box and enter the text you want to appear in that cell.

Now choose the Extended tab to view some advanced options. Here, you can set the cell alignment, the border width and colour as well as include a background image in your table.

Fig. 142. Creating a table in 1st Page.

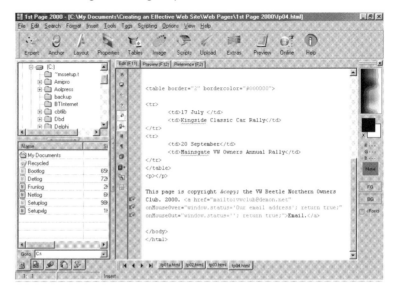

Good advice when creating tables using 1st Page 2000 is to decide on your table design, number of rows and columns and contents before you start to use the package to create the table. The HTML code that is generated makes it quite difficult to make amendments. If you make a mistake, you will probably have to start all over again.

Removing formatting, tables, and images

1st Page 2000 is a real stick-in-the-mud HTML editor. It expects you to sort out your own mistakes. If you want to remove any elements of your page the quickest way to do it is to open your HTML toolbox and get deleting. The only effective way to remove any mistakes you make is to delete them manually – refer to Part Two of this book for a crash course in HTML.

Adding links to your web page

Inserting a hyperlink
Inserting a hyperlink using 1st Page 2000 is easy. Simply click on the Anchor icon on the toolbar or choose Anchor, Link from the Insert menu. Now complete the following fields:

1. URL – the target page to be loaded when the link is pressed.

2. Description – the text to be displayed should visitors place their mouse over the link.

3. Status bar – the text to be displayed in the browser status bar.

Inserting an email link

To insert an email link, choose Email from the Insert menu. Now complete the fields as above. The only difference is that, instead of entering a URL address, you enter the email address where the message is to be directed.

Summary

1st Page 2000 is a very comprehensive HTML editing package. It covers all levels from beginner to advanced user, and encompasses a wide range of web design facilities. For the beginner, it can seem difficult to use, and the help screens confusing. However, with practice you can start finding your way around. The package offers great scope to develop your knowledge and skills.

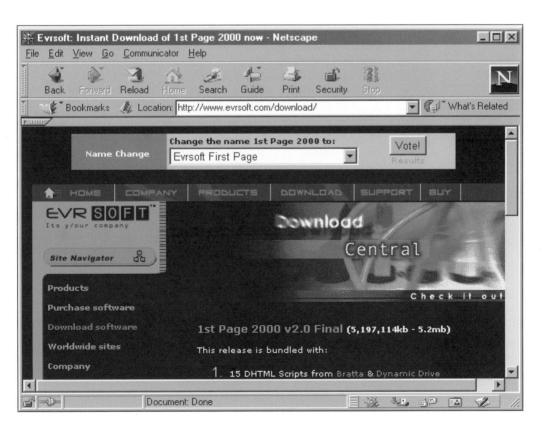

15 Using Netscape Composer

In this chapter we will explore:

▶ *introducing Netscape Composer*

▶ *creating a basic web page*

▶ *adding basic formatting*

▶ *adding an image to your web page*

▶ *adding hyperlinks and email links*

▶ *working with tables*

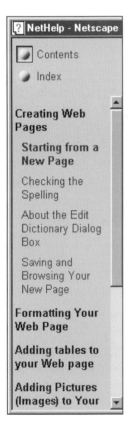

Introducing Netscape Composer

Netscape Composer is a WYSIWYG web design tool: 'what you see is what you get'. It comes free with all versions of Netscape Communicator software (Level 4.0 and above). It can also be downloaded from Netscape's home page (http://www.netscape.com). Although supplied by Netscape, web pages created using Composer can be viewed in all HTML-capable browsers, including Internet Explorer. To load Netscape Composer in a PC, choose Start, Programs, Netscape Communicator, Netscape Composer.

Creating a basic web page

To create a new page, choose the New icon on the toolbar. From here, you can choose to create a Blank Page, create your page from a Template, use the Page Wizard, or open an existing file held locally on your PC. Choose the Blank Page option. From here you can easily add and amend text, images and tables to create an effective web page, just as if you were using any word-processing software.

Saving your web pages
To save your newly created web page, click on the Save icon on the toolbar. Composer will prompt you to enter a title for your web page. This title is used by browser software and is displayed at the top of the screen once your web page is loaded. This title can be amended later by choosing the Page Colours and Properties menu option found in the Format menu.

Previewing your web page
Composer operates in a WYSYWIG environment, so the need to review your web pages is reduced. However, for safety's sake you should preview your page in a browser. This will ensure that it looks as it should for your visitors. To preview your web page, choose the Preview icon from the toolbar; your page can then be viewed in Netscape Navigator (the proprietary browser from Netscape).

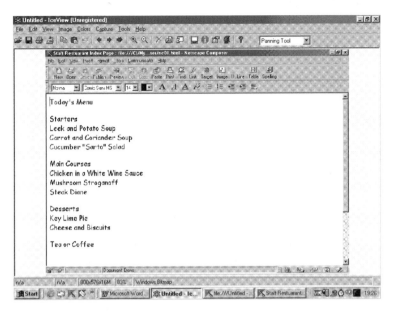

Fig. 143. A basic web page in Netscape Composer. The toolbar is clearly laid out, and offers all kinds of formatting possibilities fonts, styles and colours, page backgrounds, text alignment, tables, link creation and other features.

Opening an existing web page

To open an existing web page stored locally on your PC, choose the File Open Page option from the File menu. Now click on the Choose File button and locate and open your file. Composer is helpful here: the last working area is assumed to be the default directory so that recently used files are quickly found and loaded.

Adding basic formatting

Adding basic formatting to your web page is very easy with Netscape Composer. Suppose you want to change the font (typeface). You just highlight the text to be affected, and choose the required Font and Font

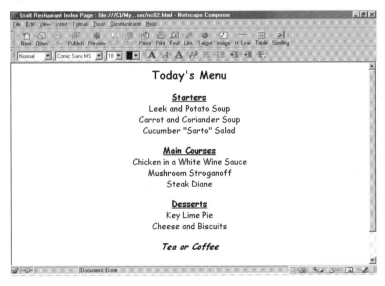

Fig. 144. Formatting a basic web page in Netscape Composer. Here, use has been made of different font sizes, centred alignment, and regular and italic text.

145

Size from the drop down boxes on the toolbar. Similarly, by selecting text and then applying Bold, Italic and Underline styles from the toolbar, you can easily enhance the look of your web page. All these options can also be found in the Format Font, Size and Style menu options.

Checking your spelling
Composer comes with a useful tool to check the spelling in your web page. From the Tools menu choose the Check Spelling option. Composer will then check the spelling throughout your document. This option is also available by pressing 'Ctrl-K'. If you just want to check part of a web page, highlight the portion of text and choose Check Spelling from the Tools menu.

Fig. 145. Character Properties in Netscape Composer. Here you can adjust the formatting of text characters, hyperlinks, paragraphs and lists.

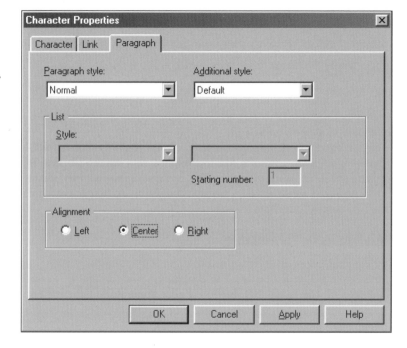

Aligning web page text
To align text within your web page, firstly highlight the text to be aligned. Then, from the Format menu, select Character Properties (figure 145). Choose the Paragraph tab and click on the required radio button to align the selected text as Left, Center or Right. You can also click on the Alignment icon on the toolbar to visually align selected text.

Changing text and background colours
There are two ways to quickly change the colour of both the text and background of your web page. To change text colour, firstly highlight the required text. Then from the Format menu choose Character Properties. Finally, click on the colour button shown, and choose and apply a new colour.

To change web page text and background colours simultaneously, from the Format menu choose the Page Colours and Properties menu item and then select the Colours and Background tab. You will now see an excellent visual point-and-click colour-changing palette. You can use it to amend the look of text, links, active links, followed links and page backgrounds.

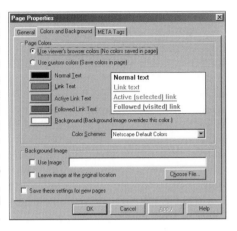

Fig. 146. Netscape Composer Page Properties. You can use this feature to select different colours for normal text, links, active links, and followed links, and to retitle your web page.

▶ *Tip* – A quick method to change the text colour is to highlight the required text and choose the appropriate colour from the drop down Font Colour box on the toolbar.

Adding symbols

Composer makes it easy to incorporate symbols and special characters into your web page. Firstly, place your cursor where you want the special symbol to go. Then, choose the Insert Special Characters menu item from within the Format menu's Character Tools option. Now choose your special character from the easy-to-read grid, and update your web page.

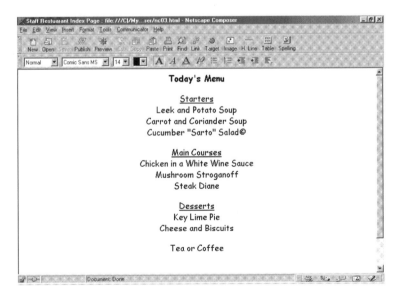

Fig. 147. A Netscape Composer web page incorporating a special character, the copyright symbol .

Working with lists

The easiest way to start a list in Netscape Composer is first to type your list. You can do it by simply typing the items in your list directly onto your web page. Now, select all of these items by highlighting them. From the Format menu, choose the List menu option. Then choose a list type from

147

Using Netscape Composer...

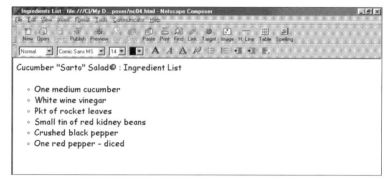

the selection provided, and watch as Composer applies the formatting to your highlighted text.

A quick way to create a bullet or numbered list is to highlight the required list text, and from the toolbar icons choose either the Bullet List or Numbered List.

Adding an image to your web page

Organising a special folder
The first suggested task will save you lots of problems once you publish your web pages onto the world wide web. It means setting up some systems defaults.

▶ *Tip* – If you're new to designing and publishing web pages, make sure that you store all your files for your complete web site in the same folder on your PC. This includes all your HTML files (i.e. your web page files) and all the graphic images displayed on these pages (GIF and JPEG files). Then, when you come to upload your site to the web, the process will be so much easier. If all the files are not stored in the same folder, complications can arise.

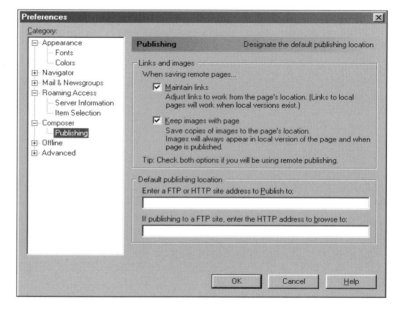

148

Composer helps you along by allowing you to set 'preferences'. For example you can ensure that any graphic image you include in your web page is stored in the same folder as the web page that you're working on. (Well, a copy of the image will be stored – no need to worry, the original will still exist.) To set this preference, choose Preferences from the Edit menu. Then click on the Composer Publishing category. Make sure the 'Keep images with page' check box is checked (figure 149).

Inserting a graphic image to your web page
To insert a graphic image into your web page, you can either click on the Image icon on the toolbar or choose Image from the Insert menu. Next, choose the file to be inserted onto your web page. From the Image Properties menu, you will see the Edit Image button. This can be used to launch the image-editing software you normally use. You can also align your image here to make sure that text wraps around it effectively, as well as choosing to use your image as a background and other formatting options. This is an excellent screen for inserting an image into your page (figure 150).

Once placed on your page, you can edit an image by right-clicking on it and choosing Image Properties. Your image can also be moved around the page by depressing the left mouse button and dragging the image to the desired position.

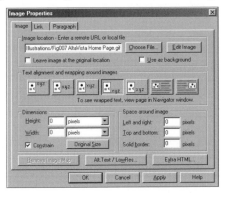

Fig. 150. The Image Properties screen in Netscape Composer. Here you can select and insert an image into your web page, set its size, and define any borders and margins. Click on the Link tab at the top, and you can easily turn the image into a hyperlink.

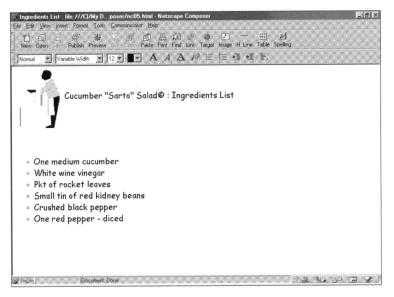

Fig. 151. An image inserted into a Netscape Composer web page. The author has made one line of text align horizontally with the picture, and placed a list beneath.

Adding hyperlinks and email links

Adding a hyperlink

To attach a hyperlink to a word or phrase in your web page, you must first select that word or phrase. With the text highlighted, right-click your mouse and choose Create Link Using Selected. Enter the page to be loaded into the Link to field, and click the OK button. The link is now created ready for use.

Fig. 152. Creating an email link in Netscape Composer. Type in the email address, remembering to prefix it with the all-important phrase 'mailto:' For example: mailto:joe@bloggs.com

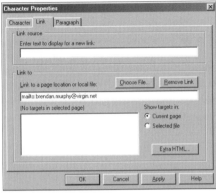

Adding an email link

To create an email link, high-light the text required to act as the link, right click as above and choose Create Link Using Selected... This time, instead of entering the name of the page to be loaded, enter a 'mailto' tag. This tag will force your visi-tor's email software to load, allowing them to send an email to you. A sample mailto expression is shown in figure 152. Such links can be also be created using the Image icon from the toolbar.

Fig. 153. The Netscape Composer web page now incorporates an email link on the last line. The link is underlined.

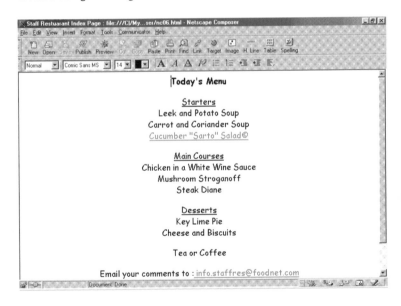

Following links

To make sure your hyperlinks are live, and result in the right internal or external web page being opened, you can try the link yourself. Right-click your mouse on the link and choose Open Link in Composer option. Check the validity of the web page that is loaded.

Working with tables

Adding a table to your web page

Tables are a good way of presenting your information in a neat and organised-looking way. It's easy to add a table to your web page. Click the Table icon on the toolbar, or choose the Table menu option from the Insert menu.

1. Enter the number of rows and columns that you want. Remember to add an extra row if you want to have column headings.

2. You can now adjust various useful table-formatting options. These include cell padding (the amount of marginal space you want between text and cell border), table alignment, and other features.

3. Once you've finished this click on OK. Start entering your text into the table much as you would do with any standard word processor or spreadsheet.

Removing table data

To delete mistakes, right-click on the table cell and choose Delete.

Formatting tables

To format a table, right-click your mouse anywhere in the table and choose the Table Properties quick menu option.

Summary

Netscape Composer is a first-class web design package that is highly functional and easy to use. It is both suitable and comprehensive for the beginner, and has very good help screens which are logically organised. The toolbar is well designed, with most functions included and clearly marked for use. Composer is an excellent web design package, and comes completely free with the browser Netscape Communicator.

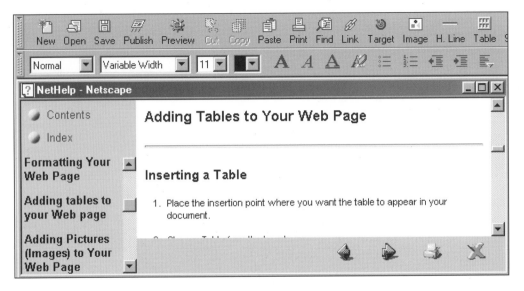

16 Using HoTMetaL PRO

In this chapter we will explore:

▶ *introducing HoTMetaL PRO*

▶ *creating a basic web page*

▶ *basic page formatting*

▶ *working with tables*

▶ *including a list in your web page*

▶ *including an image on a web page*

▶ *creating and using hyperlinks*

Introducing HoTMetaL PRO

HoTMetaL PRO is a fully functional WYSIWYG HTML editor. It is provided on a 30-day evaluation basis and can be downloaded from http://www.hotmetalpro.com

To load it from the Start menu on a PC, choose Programs, SoftQuad Applications, and HoTMetaL PRO 6.0 Eval.

Creating a basic web page

When you open HoTMetaL PRO (HMP), the main menu displays two panes. The left pane presents the Asset Manager. The right pane is blank, ready for you to display a new web page or an existing one. The Asset Manager provides you with tools to make the task of creating web pages a little easier. The Installed Assets folder displays a list of useful assets that you can use. You can use all those listed by dragging and dropping them onto your web page. It removes any need for complicated HTML code. The main Asset you are likely to use is the image library.

Fig. 154. HoTMetaL Pro's Asset Manager offers tools to make creating web pages easier. The Installed Assets folder displays a list of ones that you can use.

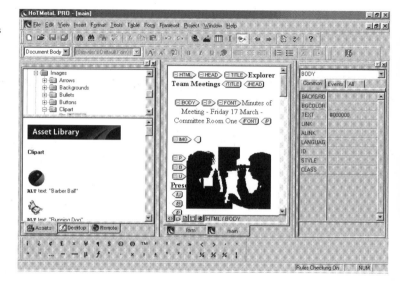

152

Creating a new web page

From the File menu, choose New Page. You could also use one of the pre-defined templates shipped with HMP. However you will make better use of these once you've mastered the basics. When you open your new page, notice that it is full of little tags. These represent the standard HTML tags used to create web pages. At first they can seem confusing, but they soon become easy to understand. In fact, they will be quite useful in helping you design your web page.

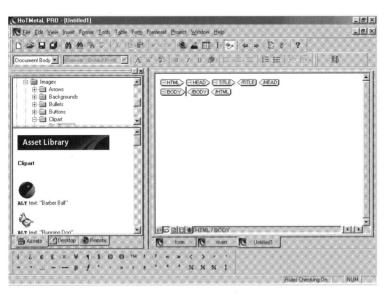

Fig. 155. A new blank page in HoTMetaLPro, showing the HTML tags in the right-hand pane.

By placing your cursor after the <TITLE> tag you can enter the page title for display in browsers. By clicking after the <BODY> tag you can begin to enter text into your web page. As your page becomes bigger, the visual tags can be expanded and contracted to suit. Clicking on the '+' or '-' sign on the desired tag will do this. Contracting the tag has no effect on the final web page. It just makes things easier to read as the page becomes more detailed and includes more information.

While you are typing in the main body text of your web page, HMP adds paragraph tags around it. To begin a new paragraph, simply click after the </P> tag and continue typing. A new paragraph will be automatically appended to your text.

Including a line break

If you want to start a new line but not a new paragraph (i.e. you don't want to include a blank line after your current line of text) then in HTML the <BR> tag is often used. To replicate this effect in HMP, place your cursor at the end of the text where the new line is to be inserted. Then press Shift-Enter or choose Insert, Element, HTML, BR.

Joining two paragraphs

You may decide that the text included in one paragraph should have been included in the previous one. In HMP it's quite easy to join two paragraphs. Place your cursor after the P tag in the second paragraph, and press the backspace key. Both paragraphs are now as a single paragraph.

Saving your web page
To save your web page, choose the Save icon from the toolbar. Alternatively, choose the Save menu option in the File menu.

Opening a web page
Once you've created some web pages using HMP you will need to open them to edit them. To do this, choose the Open icon from the toolbar, choose Ctrl-O or choose the Open menu option from the File menu. Each time you load HMP, the last web page that you've been working with is loaded.

Basic page formatting

Adding bold, italic and underline
To apply bold, italic and underline effects to text, firstly highlight the text where the effect is to be applied. Then, choose any of the three icons (bold / italic / underline) from the toolbar. Alternatively, choose these menu options from the Format menu. You will notice that HoTMetaL PRO adds the appropriate HTML tags around the selected text. To remove any of the above effects, place your cursor to the right of the opening format tag, and press the backspace key. Alternatively, select the text, click on the appropriate effect on the toolbar and the effect will now be reversed.

Aligning text
To align text on your web page, select the text and choose any of the three alignment icons from the toolbar (left / center / right). Alternatively, select the text and choose Align Left, Align Center or Align Right from the Format menu.

Changing text and background colours
To change the colour of a piece of text, firstly select that text. Then choose the Text Color icon from the toolbar or the same menu item from the Format menu. Choose your new colour, and click OK.

To change the default colours used for your web page text, backgrounds and hyperlinks choose the Page Properties menu item from the File menu. Then make any required changes. You can also create a 'custom palette' should you want to create your own colours. You can also amend the page title from within this menu option.

Inserting fractions and other symbols into your web page
To insert symbols such as fractions, currency signs and the registered trademark symbol, choose Symbols from the Insert menu. Then select the appropriate symbol from the list in the bottom panel. When you click on the symbol it is automatically inserted where your cursor is positioned in your document.

Working with tables

Adding a table to your web page

1. To add a table to your web page, choose the Insert Table icon from the toolbar.

2. Alternatively you can select the Insert Table menu item from the Table menu.

3. Enter the number of rows and columns you want for your table.

4. Choose a suitable background colour, and set some formatting options. These could include the table size, cell padding, and alignment values.

5. Look through the available tabs to decide on the overall look of your table.

6. To add data into your table, click on the NBSP character and overwrite each cell with your own information.

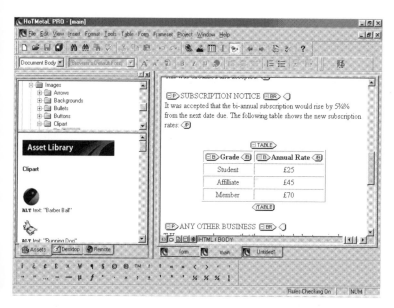

Fig. 156. Inserting a table using HoTMetaLPro.

Using the Attribute Inspector to align your table

The Attribute Inspector is an excellent tool that allows you to change the look and function of HTML tags. To call it up for your table, place your cursor to the right of the TABLE tag and right click with your mouse. Now choose the Attribute Inspector menu item, and click on the drop down menu against the ALIGN property. Change this to Center and your table will be centred in the browser window. As you begin to use HoTMetaL PRO, don't overlook the Attribute Inspector. It could save you lots of time looking for formatting tools on tags.

HoTMetaL PRO ....

Fig. 157. HoTMetaLPro includes a feature called Attribute Inspector, a handy means of changing the look and function of HTML tags.

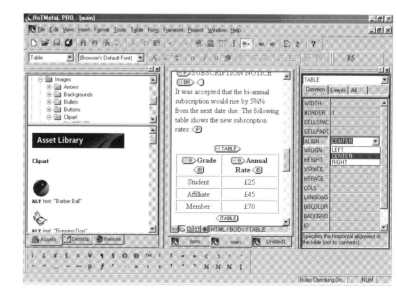

Including a list in your web page

The easiest way to include a list in your web page using HoTMetaL PRO is to place your cursor where you want to begin your list. Then choose either the Numbered List or Bulleted List icon from the toolbar. Both these options are also available from within the Format menu.

Now, just enter each item in your list, pressing the Enter key at the end of each list entry. This causes HMP to create a new list item (< LI >). Once you've completed your list, pressing the Enter key twice will close it. To change the look of your list - for example to change the style of the bullets in a bulleted list – right-click after the < UL > tag, choose the Attribute Inspector and change the list TYPE attribute.

Fig. 158. Creating a list in HoTMetaLPro.

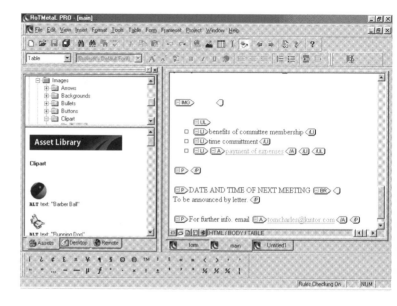

156

Including an image on a web page

To insert an image into your HoTMetaL PRO web page, you can choose the Insert Image icon from the toolbar, or choose the Image menu option from the Insert menu. Now, from the dialogue box displayed, choose the image file you want to insert. As you look through your hard disk for a suitable image an excellent preview is displayed to help you. You can also choose how text will be aligned around the image as well as setting alternate text for those browsers unable to display graphic image files.

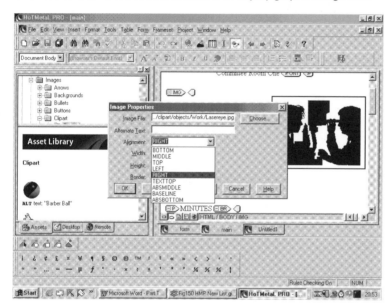

Fig. 159. Inserting and organising images in HoTMetaLPro.

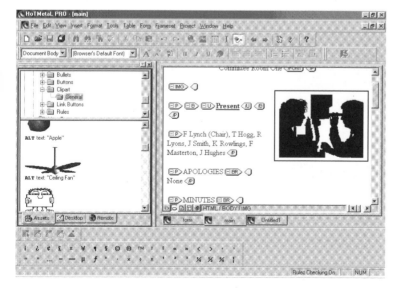

Fig. 160. The HoTMetaLPro image library.

An alternative excellent way of adding images to your web page is to use the Asset Manager shown in the left pane of your current window. From here, open the Installed Assets folder, Images, Clipart, General. Then locate a suitable graphic image. Drag and drop it into a suitable spot in your current web page as displayed in the right-hand window. HoTMetaLPro does the rest – excellent!

Creating and using hyperlinks

Adding a hyperlink

1. To insert a hyperlink in your web page, first select the text you want to act as a link.

2. Press Ctrl-K.

3. Choose the appropriate command from the Insert menu, or click on the Insert Link icon on the toolbar.

4. Enter the file or URL for the page to be loaded when the link is pressed (files are other HTML pages which are normally held locally in your web site).

If you often load pages from hyperlinks, you can create a 'hotlist' of the ones you use most often.

Adding an email link

To add an email link follow the steps outlined above. However, instead of entering a file or URL to be loaded, enter the return email address preceded with the 'mailto:' tag, as in figure 161.

Fig. 161. Creating an email link using HoTMetaLPro.

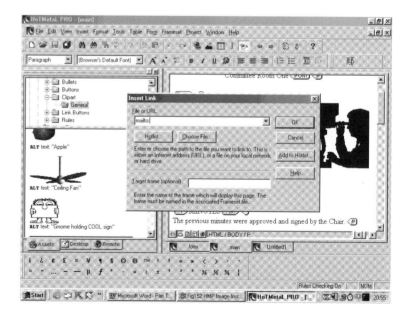

Summary

HoTMetaL PRO is a fantastic, easy-to-use and functional web design editor. It provides all the ease of use expected from a WYSIWYG editor, plus the power of raw HTML. The help screens are excellent. Using both the Asset Manager and an Attribute Inspector means you can enhance both professionalism and functionality. The package is a great tool equally suitable for a beginner and a web design expert.

17 More great web design tools

In this chapter we will explore:

▶ *Some popular web-authoring packages*

The world wide web is full of useful tools to help you build a great web site. If you've not already chosen a favourite from the packages reviewed in this book, have a look at this chapter. Here, some more of the more popular tools are discussed. Some are available as free downloads from the world wide web, some are available for a nominal registration fee. and others are full-blown commercial products and cost more to buy.

In general the web-authoring packages come with hefty paperback manuals, plus access to valuable online support. Perhaps as you develop your web-building skills you might want to move to one of these professional packages. However, using any of the web design tools listed in this part of the book, you really will be able to do 95% (and more!) of the tasks that the professionals do.

Some popular web-authoring packages

Adobe Pagemill – under £100
http://www.adobe.com
Adobe Pagemill is a WYSIWYG HTML web editor. It provides an easy route to switch design between WYSIWYG and raw HTML, so you can choose the design mode that suits you best. You will only need to know a little HTML to use Adobe Pagemill. The package comes with a comprehensive library of images, sounds and animated images that you can incorporate into your web pages. It also offers seamless links to a host of other Adobe packages such as Adobe Illustrator. Links are also provided for other popular packages such as Microsoft Word, Microsoft Photoshop and Corel Wordperfect.

Macromedia Dreamweaver – under £200
http://www.macromedia.com
Dreamweaver sits at the higher end of the marketplace for web page design tools. It is widely used by professional web designers and is a fully integrated product. It comes with templates designed to suit the needs of small business as well as ones to suit the personal user. Dreamweaver allows the creation of HTML either in WYSIWYG mode or raw HTML mode. You can watch the software actually creating the HTML while you type in WYSIWYG mode. It integrates with the excellent Fireworks Studio, which gives access to a comprehensive web image creation tool.

AOLPress – free
http://www.aolpress.com
AOLPress comes from the giant online service provider America OnLine. Although AOL provides the software, pages created using AOLPress will

work in any browser and through any internet service provider. AOLPress is a WYSIWYG editor. It suits all levels of expertise from beginner to web design expert. It isn't just a web design package, it's also a browser, allowing you to look at web pages through the software. Useful features include editable HTML, a utility to check the status of hyperlinks, and automatic built-in FTP so you can upload your finished web pages straight to the web.

Web Express – under £50
http://www.mvd.com/webexpress/
WebExpress is a very easy to use WYSIWYG HTML editor. It comes shipped with all kinds of templates. You can use these to build professional web pages easily, without the hassle of having to work in HTML. It incorporates a page creation wizard that will get you up to speed quickly and easily. Wizards are on hand to step you through table, frame and form creation. WebExpress comes with an integrated image text editor which lets you add custom text to buttons. The package also ships with built-in FTP and a handy broken links detector. You can also use the image editor launcher to load your favourite graphics package; this way you can edit your web images in a familiar environment.

Arachnophilia – free
http://www.arachnoid.com
Considering it is a free product, Arachnophilia offers a wealth of functionality and flexibility. It has an internal browser that lets you instantly preview changes as you go along. You can also toggle between six other browsers, so you are assured of designing web pages that will work in just about any environment. Arachnophilia also lets you insert pre-formatted text and tables from most Windows-compliant applications. This saves you from the often difficult formatting tasks required in HTML. The package also comes with a comprehensive spell checker and built in FTP software. Arachnophilia has excellent step-by-step tutorials on HTML, Javascript and the internet.

HomeSite – under £50
http://www.allaire.com
HomeSite is an HTML-based web design tool that seems to be a favourite with the professionals. It provides great functionality, especially in the management of attributes for specific HTML tags. Here, as you type the tag, you can choose parameters and values from a drop down list. This allows you to test the full functionality of each tag to its limit. The producers of HomeSite offer you a WYSIWYN interface (what you see is what you need). This gives you the ability to design and view browser-ready code hand in hand. A couple of wizards – table and frames wizard, and link-verification wizard – are useful. Other in-built functions allow you to check each of your hyperlinks and syntax-check your HTML code to make sure it is optimised. The package also has a great function called SiteView. This gives you a complete view of all the files that comprise your web site – invaluable once you are ready to upload your web site to the world wide web.

Allaire HomeSite Hits a Home Run
"HomeSite 4.5 is a strong candidate for developers looking to maintain a fine degree of control over their Web projects, which usually helps bring projects in on time and under budget. ... If you plan, build, and maintain Web sites for a living, HomeSite 4.5 deserves a thorough going-over."

More great web design tools . . . .

HTMLtool – nominal charge
http://www.lograf.com
This is a powerful HTML code-based web design editor. It comes complete with wizards to allow you to use complex HTML tags such as <BODY> and <FRAME>. Wizards are also on hand to help you create great looking lists and tables. HTMLtool comes with TagHelp which provides help on all tags. It also has an auto-complete function that helps you use the correct syntax when using HTML tags. A live spell checker checks and corrects as you type. A nice touch – especially if you're a computer programmer – is the ability to choose whether the default for HTML tags is lower or upper case. This allows you to apply some structure and uniformity to the web design process. HTMLtool also lets you import RTF (rich text format) files, available on most word processors. You can thus format a document in your word processor and import it direct into HTMLtool no further formatting is needed. The package also features FileWeight, which estimates how long your visitors will have to wait to load your web pages. This is invaluable if your pages include lots of graphic images or sounds. HTMLtool also comes with an excellent HTML reference guide, invaluable to the web design novice.

Hippie 98
http://www.troutsoft.com
Hippie 98 is another award-winning web design tool. A powerful HTML editor, it displays side by side on your screen both your page editing window and your local browser. This saves time constantly switching between your HTML document and your browser. Hippie 98 comes with various useful design wizards. It colour-codes HTML tags for easy identification.

Summary

When Tim-Berners Lee invented HTML in the late 1980s he never envisaged it would become the *de facto* standard for designing web pages. Indeed, he hoped that within a year someone else would come up with a way of creating web pages that was simple and accessible to all. His dream hasn't yet come true, and HTML is still the dominant element of web page design. However, lots of people have come up with lots of solutions to make the process of writing using HTML much easier.

When wondering which is the best web page tool to use, decide your main purpose for building your web site. If you are creating pages that are closed and might only be regularly accessed by a few people, content might be the most important issue. In this case you might use one of the basic HTML editor packages or you might even just use Windows Notepad and an HTML browser such as Internet Explorer.

However, if you're creating web pages for your business, or selling your skills as a web designer, you're likely to need one of the more powerful packages. This doesn't necessarily mean that you have to spend a lot of money. Many of the packages that offer good flexibility and functionality cost relatively little, and some are even free. When choosing a package for professional use, your main consideration will be support. If you need regular support to solve problems quickly, or if you regularly design advanced and complex web sites, then you might prefer a package with strong support in terms of documentation, telephone and online help.

Building web pages is tremendous fun. Whether you use the most basic package or the most complex commercial software, you'll arrive with the same result – a web site that's accessible in seconds by more than 200 million people all over the world.

It's quite a thought.

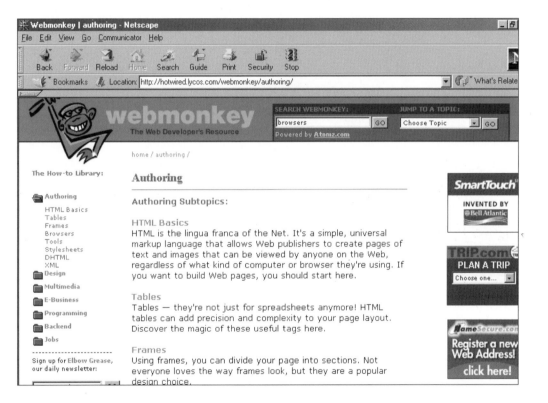

18 Managing a web project

In this chapter we will explore:

▶ *ten rules for managing a web project*
▶ *the company web site*
▶ *the personal web site*
▶ *buying a digital camera*
▶ *using a third party to design your web site*
▶ *managing a successful web site design project*

Ten rules for managing a web project

As you travel through cyberspace you'll come across things that you really like, and things you don't. The world wide web is a vast place, and millions of web pages are stored there, just waiting to be accessed by unsuspecting visitors. What is your reaction to a page that takes ages to load, is badly laid out, and has enough animated GIFs to light up Blackpool? You'll hit the back button and surf elsewhere. The web is unique in compressing the opportunity to market a product, services or personal space into a few seconds. If you lose this opportunity, customers, visitors, suppliers and others will surf away, unlikely to return. What really gets visitors to visit, stay around and return regularly, is a well designed and informative web site that meets their needs.

So, what can you do to make sure that your web pages don't end up in the 'naff' hall of fame? The following ten rules should go some way to producing the answer.

1. Go easy on the images.
2. Check your pages for grammar, spelling and punctuation.
3. Keep the page to a manageable size.
4. Send out the navigator.
5. Avoid zany colour and font combinations.
6. Avoid growing cob'webs'.
7. Regularly trawl the web for new ideas.
8. Know your visitors.
9. 'If it ain't broke don't fix it'.
10. Make sure others know about your web site.

Rule 1 — Go easy on the images!
The first and golden rule of web page design is to keep images as small as possible. On an average PC, graphics files load at a rate of about 1K per 0.75 seconds. This means that the larger the image file the longer it will take to load. Far better to use small graphics files or employ thumbnails

(small versions of the graphic which, when clicked, expand to full size).

The use of animated GIFs must also be kept within bounds. Free sites all over the web offer animated images of every subject, shape and size. Whilst they can add a certain interest to your site, do resist the temptation to make more than occasional use of them.

Remember, the content of what you say on your web page matters more than anything else. Take the case of a web site offering advice on exercise for people recovering after heart surgery. Will site visitors be more interested in the information in the text, or in the animated flashing GIFs on display? Images used on your web site are there to complement the written text so use them sparingly!

Always give your visitors the option to view your pages without images. Take a moment to change the settings on your browser to exclude the display of graphics files. Now crank up your web site in the browser: how does it look? It will probably be full of holes where the images should be, with no explanation of what is missing. Not everyone will want to display image files. Always include a text description with each image (using the ALT attribute in HTML).

Rule 2 – Check your pages for grammar, spelling and punctuation
Would you do business with an organisation whose printed literature was full of mistakes? You probably wouldn't. It's the same with web pages. It's so easy for poorly written pages to creep onto the web. When you're printing say 1,000 leaflets, the cost and time scale generally mean that few mistakes survive to the final copy. However, when you're designing on a PC and almost instantaneously displaying this work on the web, it's easy and tempting to cut corners.

When you've written the content of your web site take time to read it, and read it again. Read it out loud. Ask yourself how your visitors will read it. To ensure that your grammar and punctuation are correct, get a colleague, friend or relative to read through everything. Proof-reading is essential. In the age of spell-checkers there's no excuse for poor spelling.

Remember, your work on the web is truly global. When writing, avoid local slang. Use clear and correct English. Whilst you might understand what you're saying, visitors surfing from overseas may not. If you have to use local or dialect terms, make sure that you provide alternative meanings so that your web site is fully understandable to everyone.

Avoid using words in complete upper case. The rules of netiquette for email creation regard the use of upper case as shouting. It should be considered the same in web page writing.

Grab your visitors' attention in the first few sentences of your home page. If you don't, why would they stay? Write as clearly as you can. Use simple vocabulary, short sentences and paragraphs. Make every word count. Think of your favourite newspaper or magazine (or those of your likely visitors); select a few paragraphs and count the number of sentences in each and the number of words in each sentence. Work out an average word and sentence count for your own publication. If you adopt this same style of writing you should go a long way to making your web a success. You can assess the readability of your writing by using the Fog Index:

Managing a web project...

▶ *The Fog Index: a rough guide!* – Choose any 100-word sample from a written passage. Count the number of sentences in the sample. Include any incomplete sentences as one whole sentence. Divide 100 by the number of sentences to determine the average sentence length in terms of words. Count the number of words in the 100-word sample that have three or more syllables. Add this value to the average sentence length and multiply this figure by 0.4. This is your Fog Index for the 100-word sample. As a rule of thumb, the higher the value, then the higher the fog and the murkier your writing becomes. Aim for a Fog Index of between 6 and 11 – any higher and you've got problems. Note: the Fog Index is relative. Academic or intellectual writing might justify a higher Fog Index. Reduce the Fog Index of your web site by writing shorter sentences composed of simpler words.

Rule 3 – Keep the page to a manageable size
Your home page should act as a signpost or notice-board for your web site. Offer your visitors a table of easily readable information that directs them to the areas of interest throughout your site. Your home page shouldn't attempt much more than this. Don't try and produce a single page web site crammed with information on multiple topics.

The most effective way to organise your web site is to set up one web page per topic. This shouldn't mean keeping each page to a bare minimum in terms of content. Suppose you were giving instructions on how to change the brake pads on a Harley Davidson. Your visitors could become very frustrated by having to load, and then print, ten or eleven separate web pages. In this case it might be better to have one page, with an index of instructions at the top linking to various points ('targets') in the same page. However if each topic in your web page is fairly large then a page per topic is the way to go.

Rule 4 – Send out the navigator
Just as aircraft and ships need excellent navigational tools to travel the globe, so your web site needs tools to help your visitors travel the information superhighway. Each page on your web site should have clear links to help visitors return to previous pages or to your home page. If your pages are part of a set (maybe instructions), make sure you have 'last page', and 'next page' links to allow your visitors to move easily through the set. Also, remember to make your hypertext links clear. Your visitors should know exactly what clicking on each hypertext link will do. Finally, remember to keep your navigational links in the same place on each page. This will allow your visitors to become familiar with their location and make your web site easier to use.

Rule 5 – Avoid zany colour and font combinations
You might have highly individual tastes in colour, but don't assume that all your visitors will share them. Keep page background colours light and text dark. This contrast generally works well. Dark backgrounds look dank and cold, while bright backgrounds are more inviting. Avoid contrasting dark backgrounds with dark colour text or light backgrounds

with light text – the effect is awful. It's a good plan to use background logos or patterns only if your web site really needs it. On the whole they look amateurish and serve no purpose other than to clutter up your site and to make the text difficult to read.

It is wise to restrict the number of different fonts and font sizes. If you decide on the size and style of headings for example, apply this same style throughout your web site. Consistency of design marks the difference between amateur and professional web sites.

Rule 6 – Avoid growing cob'webs'
Cob'webs' are those dusty corners of cyberspace where no-one has visited for a very long time. Your web site will start to creak and show signs of cob'webs' unless people visit it regularly. The best way to ensure they do is: keep it up to date. Unless your site regularly features some new information, there may be little reason for anyone to return.

Rule 7 – Regularly trawl the web for new ideas
The world wide web is perfect for everyone designing both business and personal web sites. Without sending off for any company brochure, you can find out all you need in terms of style and content of web sites, simply by visiting them. Check out what's new. Is there something you've missed, or could add? How are other web sites structured and written? Is their style similar to yours? Are they likely to attract the same type of visitors?

Rule 8 – Know your visitors
To make sure that your web site meets the needs of your visitors, you must first know lots about them – their background, interests, and intellectual ability. Armed with this data you can ensure that your web site will serve its purpose. This is the true test of a web site – how well it meets the needs of its visitors.

Rule 9 – If it ain't broke don't fix it
As you travel through the world of web design you'll pick up endless new ideas, tricks and novelties. Resist at all costs the desire to build new features into your web page just for the sake of it. For example, once you've mastered HTML, you may well move on to Javascript. This doesn't mean that all your pages from then on in should be full of Javascript applets. Use new ideas and skills only where they merit being used.

Rule 10 – Make sure others know about your web site
There's no great point in having a wonderful web site, crammed with useful information, if no-one knows about it. Take the time to register your web site with all the major search engines, and ensure that you incorporate the appropriate META tags in your home page to assist these search engines. Another good way to get noticed is to network: don't be afraid to email selected other sites to request that a link be included on their links page. Perhaps you offer similar or complementary products or services – offer a reciprocal agreement to the people who help you.

Managing a web project...

The following table suggests the basic layouts for company and personal web sites:

Company web site	Personal web site
Home page	Home page
Company background/history	About you
Products/services	Guest book
Feedback form	Gallery of personal images
Gallery of product/service images	Favourite links
Links to other services	

The company web site

Home page
Company home pages should include your company logo and then detailed contact information such as your telephone number, fax number and email address (as a hypertext link). You might also include the international dialling code for your business should overseas visitors call. Everything else that is included here is really up to you. Generally it's better to keep the page clean and crisp, and use it mainly as a signpost to the rest of your site.

If you do decide to include more information here, restrict it to meaningful and clear detail about the services your company offers. This is your opportunity to market your main selling points, and say why customers should choose to do business with you. This is your last chance to make a first impression! Any words relating to your services might have hypertext links to the relevant pages on your site. You might include a link to any current special offers that your company is promoting.

It could also be a good idea to include on your home page details of any awards you have won, or any professional bodies to which you belong, or even details about any charitable causes that your organisation supports.

Company background/history
This page can be a straightforward account of your company's history and evolution. When writing it ask yourself why potential customers would click here. They are probably seeking some assurance of credibility and this might affect their decision whether or not to do business with you. It is important to give this page the right air of self-confidence and maturity.

Products/services
This part of your web site is likely to consist of more than one page. Try organising your products or services into categories, and put each category on a separate web page. Make sure your visitors have as much information as possible against each product or service – appropriate images, product/service specifications, and product/service costs.

Feedback form
Many sites on the web have feedback forms that harvest a wealth of information about visitors. Feedback forms can be difficult for visitors to complete, especially if they don't have good typing skills, or if English is not their first language. Just ask for a minimal amount of information. By their very presence here, visitors are showing that they wish to discuss their requirements. A good feedback form might just ask for their name, company name, telephone number, fax number, email address and comment or query.

Gallery of products/services
It is often said that 'a picture paints a thousand words'. In web-speak it might be better to say: 'a *small* picture paints a thousand words!' This page in your web site should include pictures of your products or services. Never forget how long it takes to load an image. Keep your images small, and to the point. Visitors will want to see what you can do; concentrate on images that highlight your products/services. Action shots (maybe someone using one of your products) are far more eye-catching than inanimate shots.

Links to other services
Take the opportunity to use this page as a tool for networking with organisations complementary to your own. Agree to include links to their home page if they will do the same for you.

The personal web site

Home page
Personal home pages should be less formal than business pages. However, the concept of 'small is beautiful' should still apply. Firstly, give your contact details here – address, telephone number and email address. Include a friendly welcoming message and logo, and maybe even a small picture of yourself or your family. You could also include a site counter letting you know the number of visitors that your home page attracts. Include some text relating to your site contents, keeping an informal mood. Perhaps your personal site doubles as a work-related site (maybe you're a self-employed professional, or a teacher who leaves resources for students/parents on your site). If so, try to make sure that you cater for the needs of friends and business visitors alike, though this may be difficult to achieve.

About you
On this page give your visitors an overview of who you are and what you do. You might include details such as your age, where you were raised, the make-up of your family, your education and your job. You could also include more light-hearted information such as your star sign, favourite food and favourite performing artist.

Guest book
The structure of your guest book should be kept simple. Most people will

just want to say a quick hello. Limit the guest book fields to details such as name, email address and a comment.

Gallery of personal images

In a personal gallery, visitors should really get a feel for you as a person by looking at the photographs on display. Make good use of this page to show pictures of your family, your friends, your hobbies and your favourite holiday snaps. Include family events such as marriage and birthday celebrations. As previously mentioned, keep the images small. If necessary, arrange this gallery across a number of web pages.

Favourite links

In this page, include links to sites that interest you. If your site is mainly set up for use by family and friends, or if a visitor chances upon it and decides to stay, your likes could well match theirs. Include links to plenty of sites you've encountered on your travels across the web. Include a 'surprise link' that would amaze your friends and family, and create a talking point.

Understanding reading patterns

It's worth remembering the way people read. We generally browse a page in a 'Z' pattern, starting from the top left, and moving through the 'Z' pattern to the bottom right of the screen. Most of our absorption is at the start of our reading, with the least at the end of the process. If you want your message to be absorbed make sure it's in the top half of the screen.

Using a digital camera

You may well want to put photographs on your web site. Many companies now offer standard 35mm photographs back on CD format after development. However, the most flexible way to acquire photographs for your web site is to use a digital camera and download them straight to your PC.

The proliferation of digital cameras means that many now come with a whole range of extras. For example, you can buy a camera that allows audio recordings to be made against each image captured (allowing you to remember what or who you are photographing). You can have a remote control, and you can even have a camera with a rotatable lens so you can take a self portrait. When you're buying a camera for web use, the key is simplicity. The web doesn't yet have the capability to display very detailed images (due to the size of these images and their speed to load). Your needs will be perfectly well covered by cameras in the basic price range. The following checklist should help you choose the best product for your needs:

Checklist for buying a digital camera

1. Storage space – Make sure that the camera you choose can store at least 50 images at the highest storage resolution. This allows you greater flexibility when taking lots of photographs.

2. Battery life – Buy a camera with both a rechargeable battery and mains operation. Make sure that the camera will operate for over an hour when fully charged.

3. Size – Buy the smallest camera that meets your requirements, so it can be carried in your pocket.

4. Ease of download – If you download images from a digital camera to your PC you'll want it to be as easy as possible. For complete ease of use – buy a camera that takes a floppy disk this allows you to transfer the image using the PC floppy drive. Alternatively ensure that the camera downloads as fast as possible using either a serial, parallel or SCSI cable. Cameras that download via a cable are the most popular.

5. Optical zoom – An optical zoom is preferable to a digital zoom. An optical zoom gives a far clearer picture when zoomed images are displayed. Look for an optical zoom of at least 3 times the original size of the image (X3). Digital zooms are also fine if your budget doesn't stretch to an optical zoom lens.

6. Viewer – The viewer allows you to see the photograph about to be taken. LCD (liquid crystal display) viewers give you a bigger real-time area to view, like a camcorder, but they use up battery life rapidly. An optical viewfinder lets you view the photograph through the traditional 35mm camera means.

7. Ease of use – Most digital cameras come with very easy-to-use instructions. At the very least ensure that your camera lets you delete stored photographs and change the resolution of photographs being taken, so you can determine the quality of the image

Using a third party to design your web site

Over the past few years, the number of companies offering web site design has increased dramatically. These companies generally fall into one of two camps:

(a) software and IT computer companies
(b) design and marketing companies

Web-site design requires a combination of skills. There are the technical skills required to understand HTML, uploading pages, URLs and other such tasks, and there are the design skills needed to make the site look professional and interesting. Many software companies now employ graphic designers to handle the look of web pages, whilst many design and marketing companies now employ technical programmers to write the HTML (and other technical tasks) to do with the site.

So, what type of company do you choose? The answer probably lies in your needs. If you're looking to have a straightforward site (in terms of design) then you'll be best placed to stick with the software company. However, expect to take a big role in deciding how the site will look. If you're really looking to impress then you might be best placed using a design and marketing company. In the end, the only way to make the right decision is to ask to see each company's work. This, coupled with the price charged, will help you make up your mind.

Finding web site design companies

There are a number of ways to go about finding a web site design company. Firstly, you could look for 'web design' using one of the search engines. However, do limit your search, or you'll have literally thousands of sites to sift through. You could also look at web pages that impress you and look for any clues as to the identity of the developer on the site. You might find a link near the bottom of the page which will take you straight to their site. You might also try searching through the companies listed in the UK Web Design Directories (http://www.webdesign.co.uk) or those companies who are members of the British Web Design and Marketing Association (http://www.bwdma.co.uk). You could also use more traditional methods such as browsing through Yellow Pages and calling the companies listed there.

Finally, if you're on a tight budget you might consider phoning your local college to see whether any smart student can help you out with some work placement. The great thing about commissioning a web site is that it doesn't have to be a local company. If you find the best deal from a company based in a beach shack on the Eastern Seaboard of the USA, then as long as you're armed with a browser and a credit card you need never meet and you can still do rewarding and effective business with them.

Ensure that your needs are going to be met

Once you've chosen a company or an individual to design your site the next thing is to brief them on what you require. If your web site is large enough, at this point you could request companies to come forward with ideas in a competitive bid environment. Whatever size your web site is, make sure that the designers understand your business. This means arranging a visit to your work environment to let them get a feel for your organisation. The culture, the dress policy, the type of customers you have, any business awards, how the phones are answered, the photograph and pictures in the reception area – all of these environmental factors give a feel for your organisation. A good designer should be able to draw on this to good advantage when building a web site. You must then visit the designer's premises and see their work environment and ask to see current projects, sample web sites, customer testimonials. Check whether they've done similar work in your area of business for other clients. Try to find some synergy with your business needs.

Agreeing a contract

Before you agree a contract and a fee make sure that the following points are clearly understood:

1. The time scale for the project is clearly stated and can be achieved.

2. The company completely understands your requirements.

3. The company agrees to regular update meetings including periodic reviews of the web site as it is being built.

4. The cost is agreed and is fixed. Ensure that you will not be asked to pay any more than initially agreed.

5. Check for any annual maintenance charges and agree charges for up-dating your pages.

Managing your web site design project
Commissioning a web site from an external supplier is no different from commissioning someone to build you a new conservatory for your home, or design a new air conditioning system for your office building. The same principles of project management apply. The following guidelines on designing the content of your web site, and the guide to project steps, should be followed when managing a web design project.

Setting down your requirements on paper
The best way to design your web site is to create a 'storyboard' using A4 paper. For each 'page' of your web site, use a 'page' of blank paper. Add a heading and bullet point list of what you want covered on that page. For each bullet point write the text needed to expand the bullet (remembering to watch out for grammar, spelling and punctuation). Then, include a list of any navigational links needed to link the page with other pages on your site and with your home page. List any other links to other sites on the web. Attach any photographs or images that might need scanned or a disk with images for the page. Include an index sheet to allow easy identification of each page. There you have it, the bulk of your web site down on paper ready for your web site designer.

Managing a successful web site design project

Here are four key elements in making sure your project is a success:

1. *Set up a project team* – This team should be made of individuals with an interest in the concept or content of your web site. This group should plan out on paper a draft project plan detailing the key points in the project and the overall project time scales.

2. *Agree the project plan with your web site designer* – Submit your draft plan to your web site designer and gain his or her agreement. At this stage some negotiation of time scales may be expected.

3. *Ensure milestones are reached* – Project milestones are points in the lifetime of a project where a major part of the project should be completed and ready for review. Ensure that milestones are set and that regular review meetings determine whether they are being met. Include online reviews where you (and maybe even your customers) can review the current state of the site being designed.

4. *Set up regular project meetings* – The key to success of your project will be regular communication between you and your web site design company. These meetings will give you and your designers the chance to clarify any points and note successes/failures during the project.

Managing a web project..

The above steps, if followed, should ensure that you keep tight control over the design of your web site. You might think that the whole process seems rigid and bureaucratic. However, technological projects (and 'techie' people) are notorious for over-running time scales and budgets, so a well-structured plan will minimise the risks. Also, don't pay for the site until you are completely happy. If you feel that the project isn't going the way you envisaged, don't be afraid to take tough decisions such as delaying or abandoning the project altogether.

Questions and answers

Should I buy a digital camera to use with my web site?
Unless your site is principally text-based then the answer is probably yes. Digital images, when used correctly, enhance the look and feel of your web site.

Do I need to employ a specialised design company to design my web site?
No. Web sites can be designed by professional design and marketing companies, by software companies, educational establishments and individuals. Choose the right supplier according to what you need.

Case studies

Tom decides to go it alone
Tom has recently left his company where he was an analyst/programmer. Over the last two years he has specialised in the design of company web sites. He is now setting up as a small independent company offering web page design to community businesses. Tom feels that his offer of a standard price for a four-page web site will attract budget-conscious customers.

Kenny needs a new shop window
Kenny has sold art from his premises in Keswick for the last 15 years. Over this time the number of American tourists purchasing Kenny's work has risen steadily, until at present over 40% of his turnover comes from this group. Kenny has decided to commission a web site to allow these visitors to keep in touch and view some of the prints on sale in his shop, and maybe even purchase them online. Kenny has asked whether his present marketing company can help. To his surprise they have recently employed a computer programmer, and together with their existing graphic designer it means that Kenny's needs can be fully met.

Glossary of internet terms

access provider – The company that provides you with access to the internet. This may be an independent provider or a large international organisation such as AOL or CompuServe. See also **internet service provider.**

ActiveX – A programming language that allows effects such as animations, games and other interactive features to be included a web page.

Adobe Acrobat – A type of software required for reading PDF files ('portable document format'). You may need to have Adobe Acrobat Reader when downloading large text files from the internet, such as lengthy reports or chapters from books. If your computer lacks it, the web page will prompt you, and usually offer you an immediate download of the free version.

address book – A directory in a web browser where you can store people's email addresses. This saves having to type them out each time you want to email someone. You just click on an address whenever you want it.

AltaVista – One of the half dozen most popular internet search engines. Just type in a few key words to find what you want on the internet: http://www.altasvista.com

anchor – Marked text that indicates a hypertext link

AOL – America OnLine, the world's biggest internet service provider, with more than 20 million subscribers, and now merged with Time Warner. Because it has masses of content of its own - quite aside from the wider internet - it is sometimes referred to as an 'online' service provider rather than internet service provider. It has given away vast numbers of free CDs with the popular computer magazines to build its customer base.

applet – An application programmed in Java that is designed to run only on a web browser. Applets cannot read or write data onto your computer, only from the domain in which they are served from. When a web page using an applet is accessed, the browser will download it and run it on your computer. See also **Java.**

application – Any program, such as a word processor or spreadsheet program, designed for use on your computer.

ARPANET – Advanced Research Projects Agency Network, an early form of the internet.

ASCII – American Standard Code for Information Interchange. It is a simple text file format that can be accessed by most word processors and text editors. It is a universal file type for passing textual information across the internet.

Ask Jeeves – A popular internet search engine. Rather than just typing in a few key words for your search, you can type in a whole question or instruction, such as 'Find me everything about online investment.' It draws on a database of millions of questions and answers, and works best with fairly general questions.

ASP – Active Server Pages, a filename extension for a type of web page.

attachment – A file sent with an email message. The attached file can be anything from a word-processed document to a database, spreadsheet, graphic, or even a sound or video file. For example you could email someone birthday greetings, and attach a sound track or video clip.

Glossary ···

Authenticode – Authenticode is a system where ActiveX controls can be authenticated in some way, usually by a certificate.

avatar – A cartoon or image used to represent someone on screen while taking part in internet chat.

backup – A second copy of a file or a set of files. Backing up data is essential if there is any risk of data loss.

bandwidth – The width of the electronic highway that gives you access to the internet. The higher the bandwidth, the wider this highway, and the faster the traffic can flow.

banner ad – This is a band of text and graphics, usually situated at the top of a web page. It acts like a title, telling the user what the content of the page is about. It invites the visitor to click on it to visit that site. Banner advertising has become big business.

baud rate – The data transmission speed in a modem, measured in bps (bits per second).

BBS – Bulletin board service. A facility to read and to post public messages on a particular web site.

binary numbers – The numbering system used by computers. It only uses 1s and 0s to represent numbers. Decimal numbers are based on the number 10. You can count from nought to nine. When you count higher than nine, the nine is replaced with a 10. Binary numbers are based on the number 2: each place can only have the value of 1 or 0. You can count from nought to one. When you count higher than one, the one is replaced by 10 (not ten but one zero). Binary 10 would be equal to Decimal 2. For example:

Decimal	0	1	2	3	4	5	6	7	8	9	10
Binary	0	1	10	11	100	101	110	111	1000	1001	1010

Blue Ribbon Campaign – A widely supported campaign supporting free speech and opposing moves to censor the internet by all kinds of elected and unelected bodies.

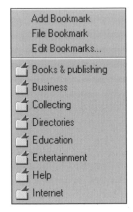

bookmark – A file of URLs of your favourite internet sites. Bookmarks are very easily created by bookmarking (mouse-clicking) any internet page you like the look of. If you are an avid user, you could soon end up with hundreds of them! In the Internet Explorer browser and AOL they are called 'favourites'.

boolean search – A search in which you type in words such as AND and OR to refine your search. Such words are called 'Boolean operators'. The concept is named after George Boole, a nineteenth-century English mathematician.

bot – Short for robot. It is used to refer to a program that will perform a task on the internet, such as carrying out a search.

browser – Your browser is your window to the internet, and will normally supplied by your internet service provider when you first sign up. It is the program that you use to access the world wide web, and manage your personal communications and privacy when online. By far the two most popular browsers are Netscape Communicator and its dominant rival Microsoft Internet Explorer. You can easily swap. Both can be downloaded free from their web sites and are found on the CD roms stuck to the computer magazines. It won't make much difference which one you use - they both do much the same thing. Opera, at http://www.opera.com is a great alternative that improves security, is faster and more efficient.

bug – A weakness in a program or a computer system.

bulletin board – A type of computer-based news service that provides an email service and a file archive.

cache – A file storage area on a computer. Your web browser will normally cache (copy to your hard drive) each web page you visit. When you revisit that page on the web, you may in fact be looking at the page originally cached on your computer. To be sure you are viewing the current page, press **reload** – or **refresh** – on your browser toolbar. You can empty your cache from time to time, and the computer will do so automatically whenever the cache is full. In Internet Explorer, pages are saved in the Windows folder, Temporary Internet Files. In Netscape they are saved in a folder called 'cache'.

certificate – A computer file that securely identifies a person or organisation on the internet.

CGI (common gateway interface) – This defines how the web server should pass information to the program, such as what it's being asked to do, what objects it should work with, any inputs, and so on. It is the same for all web servers.

channel (chat) – Place where you can chat with other internet chatters. The name of a chat channel is prefixed with a hash mark, #.

click through – This is when someone clicks on a banner ad or other link, for example, and is moved from that page to the advertiser's web site.

client – This is the term given to the program that you use to access the internet. For example your web browser is a web client, and your email program is an email client.

community – The internet is often described as a net community. This refers to the fact that many people like the feeling of belonging to a group of like-minded individuals. Many big web sites have been developed along these lines, such as GeoCities which is divided into special-interest 'neighbour-hoods', or America OnLine which is strong on member services.

compression – Computer files can be electronically compressed, so that they can be uploaded or downloaded more quickly across the internet, saving time and money. If an image file is compressed too much, there may be a loss of quality. To read them, you uncompress 'unzip' them.

content – Articles, columns, sales messages, images, and the text of your web site.

content services – Web sites dedicated to a particular subject.

cookie – A cookie is a small code that the server asks your browser to keep until it asks for it. If it sends it with the first page and asks for it back before each other page, they can follow you around the site, even if you switch your computer off in between.

cracker – Someone who breaks into computer systems with the intention of causing some kind of damage or abusing the system in some way.

crash – What happens when a computer program malfunctions. The operating system of your PC may perform incorrectly or come to a complete stop ('freeze'), forcing you to shut down and restart.

cross-posting – Posting an identical message in several different newsgroups at the same time.

cybercash – This is a trademark, but is also often used as a broad term to describe the use of small payments made over the internet using a new form of electronic account that is loaded up with cash. You can send this money to the companies offering such cash facilities by cheque, or by credit card.

Some internet companies offering travel-related items can accept electronic cash of this kind.

cyberspace – Popular term for the intangible 'place' where you go to surf - the ethereal and borderless world of computers and telecommunications on the internet.

cypherpunk – From the cypherpunk mailing list charter: 'Cypherpunks assume privacy is a good thing and wish there were more of it. Cypherpunks acknowledge that those who want privacy must create it for themselves and not expect governments, corporations, or other large, faceless organisations to grant them privacy out of beneficence. Cypherpunks know that people have been creating their own privacy for centuries with whispers, envelopes, closed doors, and couriers. Cypherpunks do not seek to prevent other people from speaking about their experiences or their opinions.'

cypherpunk remailer – Cypherpunk remailers strip headers from the messages and add new ones.

data – Information. Data can exist in many forms such as numbers in a spreadsheet, text in a document, or as binary numbers stored in a computer's memory.

dial up account – This allows you to connect your computer to your internet provider's computer remotely.

digital – Based on the two binary digits, 1 and 0. The operation of all computers is based on this amazingly simple concept. All forms of information are capable of being digitalised - numbers, words, and even sounds and images - and then transmitted over the internet.

Dial-Up Networking

directory – On a PC, a folder containing your files.

DNS – Domain name server.

domain name – A name that identifies an IP address. It identifies to the computers on the rest of the internet where to access particular information. Each domain has a name. For someone@somewhere.co.uk, 'somewhere' is the domain name. The domain name for Internet Handbooks for instance is: www.internet-handbooks.co.uk

DotUK – One of the largest UK 'talkers'.

download – 'Downloading' means copying a file from one computer on the internet to your own computer. You do this by clicking on a button that links you to the appropriate file. Downloading is an automatic process, except you have to click 'yes' to accept the download and give it a file name. You can download any type of file - text, graphics, sound, spreadsheet, computer programs, and so on.

ebusiness – The broad concept of doing business to business, and business to consumer sales, over the internet.

ecash – Short for electronic cash. See cybercash.

ecommerce – The various means and techniques of transacting business online.

email – Electronic mail, any message or file you send from your computer to another computer using your 'email client' program (such as Netscape Messenger or Microsoft Outlook).

email address – The unique address given to you by your ISP. It can be used by others using the internet to send email messages to you. An example of a standard email address is: mybusiness@aol.com

email bomb – An attack by email where you are sent hundreds or thousands of email messages in a very short period. This attack often prevents you from receiving genuine email messages.

emoticons – Popular symbols used to express emotions in email, for example the smiley :-) which means 'I'm smiling. Emoticons are not normally appropriate for business communications.

encryption – The scrambling of information to make it unreadable without a key or password. Email and any other data can now be encrypted using PGP and other freely available programs. Modern encryption has become so amazingly powerful as to be to all intents and purposes uncrackable. Law enforcers world wide are pressing their governments for access to people's and organisation's passwords and security keys. Would you be willing to hand over yours?

Excite – A popular internet directory and search engine used to find pages relating to specific keywords which you enter. See also Yahoo!.

ezines – The term for magazines and newsletters published on the internet.

FAQ – Frequently asked questions. You will see 'FAQ' everywhere you go on the internet. If you are ever doubtful about anything check the FAQ page, if the site has one, and you should find the answers to your queries.

favorites – The rather coy term for **bookmarks** – used by Internet Explorer, and by America Online. Maintaining a list of 'favourites' is designed to make returning to a site easier.

file – A file is any body of data such as a word processed document, a spreadsheet, a database file, a graphics or video file, sound file, or computer program.

filtering software – Software loaded onto a computer to prevent access by someone to unwelcome content on the internet, notably porn. The well-known 'parental controls' include CyberSitter, CyberPatrol, Surf-Watch and NetNanny. They can be blunt instruments. For example, if they are programmed to reject all web pages containing the word 'virgin', you would not be able to access any web page hosted at Richard Branson's Virgin Net! Of course, there are also web sites that tell you step-by-step how to disable or bypass these filtering tools.

finger – A tool for locating people on the internet. The most common use is to see if a person has an account at a particular internet site. Also, a chat command which returns information about the other chat user, including idle time (time since they last did anything).

firewall – A firewall is special security software designed to stop the flow of certain files into and out of a computer network, e.g. viruses or attacks by hackers. A firewall would be an important feature of any fully commercial web site.

flame – A more or less hostile or aggressive message posted in a newsgroup or to an individual newsgroup user. If they get out of hand there can be flame wars.

folder – The name for a directory on a computer. It is a place in which files are stored.

form – A web page that allows or requires you to enter information into fields on the page and send the information to a web site, program or individual on the web. Forms are often used for registration or sending questions and comments to web sites.

forums – Places for discussion on the internet. They include Usenet newsgroups, mailing lists, and bulletin board services.

frames – A web design feature in which web pages are divided into several areas or panels, each containing separate information. A typical set of frames in a page includes an index frame (with navigation links), a banner

Glossary ....

frame (for a heading), and a body frame (for text matter).

freebies – The 'give away' products, services or other enticements offered on a web site to attract registrations.

freespace – An allocation of free web space by an internet service provider or other organisation, to its users or subscribers.

freeware – Software programs made available without charge. Where a small charge is requested, the term is **shareware**.

front page – The first page of your web site that the visitor will see. Front-Page is also the name of a popular web authoring package from Microsoft.

FTP – File transfer protocol the method the internet uses to speed files back and forth between computers. Your browser will automatically select this method, for instance, when you want to download your bank statements to reconcile your accounts. In practice you don't need to worry about FTP unless you are thinking about creating and publishing your own web pages: then you would need some of the freely available FTP software. Despite the name, it's easy to use.

GIF – 'Graphic interchange format', a very common type of graphic file. It is a compressed file format used on web pages and elsewhere to display files that contain graphic images. See also JPEG.

graphical client – A graphical client typically uses many windows, one for each conversation you are involved in. Each window has a command line and status bar.

GUI – Short for graphic user interface. It describes the user-friendly screens found in Windows and other WIMP environments (Windows, icons, mice, pointers).

hacker – A person interested in computer programming, operating systems, the internet and computer security. The term can be used to describe a person who breaks into computer systems with the intention of pointing out the weaknesses in a system. In common usage, the term is often wrongly used to describe crackers.

header – The header is that part of a message which contains information about the sender and the route that the message took through the internet.

history list – A record of visited web pages. Your browser probably includes a history list. It is handy way of revisiting sites whose addresses you have forgotten to bookmark - just click on the item you want in the history list. You can normally delete all or part of the history list in your browser. However, your ISP may well be keeping a copy of this information (see **internet service providers**).

hit counter – A piece of software used by a web site to publicly display the number of hits it has received.

hits – The number of times a web page has been viewed.

home page – This refers to the index page of an individual or an organisation on the internet. It usually contains links to related pages of information, and to other relevant sites.

host – A host is the computer where a particular file or domain is located, and from where people can retrieve it.

HotBot – A popular internet search engine used to find pages relating to any keywords you decide to enter.

HTML – Hyper text markup language, the universal computer language used to create pages on the world wide web. It is much like word processing, but uses special 'tags' for formatting the text and creating hyperlinks to other web pages.

HTTP – Hypertext transfer protocol, the protocol used by the world wide web. It is the language spoken between your browser and the web servers. It is the standard way that HTML documents are transferred from host computer to your local browser when you're surfing the internet. You'll see this acronym at the start of every web address, for example:

http://www.abcxyz.com

With modern browsers, it is no longer necessary to enter 'http://' at the start of the address.

hyperlink – See **link.**

hypertext – This is a link on an HTML page that, when clicked with a mouse, results in a further HTML page or graphic being loaded into view on your browser.

Infoseek – One of the ten most popular internet search engines.

internet – The broad term for the fast-expanding network of global computers that can access each other in seconds by phone and satellite links. If you are using a modem on your computer, you too are part of the internet. The general term 'internet' encompasses email, web pages, internet chat, newsgroups, and video conferencing. It is rather like the way we speak of 'the printed word' when we mean books, magazines, newspapers, newsletters, catalogues, leaflets, tickets and posters. The 'internet' does not exist in one place any more than 'the printed word' does.

internet account – The account set up by your internet service provider which gives you access to the world wide web, electronic mail facilities, newsgroups and other value added services.

Internet Explorer – The world's most popular browser software, a product of MicroSoft and leading the field against Netscape (now owned by America OnLine).

internet service providers – ISPs are commercial, educational or official organisations which offer people ('users') access to the internet. The well-known commercial ones in the UK include AOL, CompuServe, BT Internet, Freeserve, Demon and Virgin Net. Commercial ISPs may levy a fixed monthly charge, though the worldwide trend is now towards free services. Services typically include access to the world wide web, email and newsgroups, as well as others such as news, chat, and entertainment. Your internet service provider will know everything you do on the internet - emails sent and received, web sites visited, information downloaded, key words typed into search engines, newsgroups visited and messages read and posted. This is why many of them are willing to offer their services free. What do they do with all this data? How long do they store it? Do they make it discreetly available to enforcement agencies? Do they allow the police private access? There are some major issues of personal privacy and data protection in all this, at both a national and European level, and state surveillance is expanding fast. At the very least, check out your service provider's privacy statement but it may mean very little.

Internic – The body responsible for allocating and maintaining internet domain names: http://www.internic.net

intranet – A private computer network that uses internet technology to allow communication between individuals, for example within a large commercial organisation. It often operates on a LAN (local area network).

IP address – An 'internet protocol' address. All computers linked to the internet have one. The address is somewhat like a telephone number, and consists of four sets of numbers separated by dots.

IRC – Internet relay chat. Chat is an enormously popular part of the internet, and there are all kinds of chat rooms and chat software. The chat involves typing messages which are sent and read in real time. It was developed in 1988 by a Finn called Jarkko Oikarinen.

ISDN – Integrated Services Digital Network. This is a high-speed telephone network that can send computer data from the internet to your PC faster than a normal telephone line.

Java – A programming language developed by Sun Microsystems to use the special properties of the internet to create graphics and multimedia applications on web sites.

JavaScript – A simple programming language that can be put onto a web page to create interactive effects such as buttons that change appearance when you position the mouse over them.

jpeg – The acronym is short for Joint Photographic Experts Group. A JPEG is a specialised file format used to display graphics files on the internet. JPEG files are smaller than similar GIF files and so have become ever more popular – even though there is sometimes a feeling that their quality is not as good as GIF format files. See also MPEG.

key shortcut – Two keys pressed at the same time. Usually the 'control' key (Ctrl), 'Alt' key, or 'Shift' key combined with a letter or number. For example to use 'Control-D', press 'Control', tap the 'D' key once firmly then take your finger off the 'Control' key.

keywords – Words that sum up your web site for being indexed in search engines. For example for a cosmetic site the key words might include beauty, lipstick, make-up, fashion, cosmetic and so on.

kick – To eject someone from a chat channel.

LAN – A local area network, a computer network usually located in one building or campus.

link – A hypertext phrase or image that calls up another web page when you click on it. Most web sites have lots of hyperlinks, or 'links' for short. These appear on the screen as buttons, images or bits of text (often underlined) that you can click on with your mouse to jump to another site on the world wide web.

Linux – A new widely and freely available operating system for personal computers, and a potentially serious challenger to Microsoft. It has developed a growing following.

listserver – An automated email system whereby subscribers are able to receive and send email from other subscribers to the list.

log on – You may be asked to 'log on' to certain sites and particular pages. This normally means entering your user ID in the form of a name and a password.

log on/log off – To access/leave a network. In the early days of computing this literally involved writing a record in a log book.

lurk – The slang term used to describe reading a newsgroup's messages without actually taking part in that newsgroup. Despite the connotations of the word, it is a perfectly respectable activity on the internet.

macros – 'Macro languages' are used to automate repetitive tasks in Word processors.

mail server – A remote computer that enables you to send and receive emails. Your internet access provider will usually act as your mail server.

mailing list – A forum where messages are distributed by email to the mem-

bers of the forum. The two types of lists are discussion and announcement. Discussion lists allow exchange between list members. Announcement lists are one-way only and used to distribute information such as news or humour. A good place to find mailing lists is Liszt (http://www.liszt.com). You can normally quit a mailing list by sending an email message to request removal.

marquee – A moving (scrolling) line of text, banner or other graphic on a web site, normally used for advertising purposes.

Media Player – Software on a personal computer that will play sounds and images including video clips and animations.

metasearch engine – A site that sends a keyword search to many different search engines and directories so you can use many search engines from one place.

meta tags – The technical term for the keywords used in your web page code to help search engine software rank your site.

Mixmaster – An anonymous remailer that sends and receives email messages as packages of exactly the same size and often randomly varies the delay time between receiving and remailing to make interception harder.

modem – This is an internal or external piece of hardware plugged into your PC. It links into a standard phone socket, thereby giving you access to the internet. The word derives from MOdulator/DEModulator.

moderator – A person in charge of a mailing list, newsgroup or forum. The moderator prevents unwanted messages.

mpeg – or **mpg** – The file format used for video clips available on the internet. See also JPEG.

MP3 – An immensely popular audio format that allows you to download and play music on your computer. It compresses music to create files that are small yet whose quality is almost as good as CD music. See http://mpeg.org for further technical information, or the consumer web site www.mp3.com. At time of writing, MP4, even faster to download was being developed.

MUDs – Multi-User Dungeons, interactive chat-based fantasy world games. Popular in the early days of the internet, they are in now in decline with the advance of networked arcade games such as Quake and Doom.

navigate – To click on the hyperlinks on a web site in order to move to other web pages or internet sites.

net – A slang term for the internet. In the same way, the world wide web is often just called the web.

netiquette – Popular term for the unofficial rules and language people follow to keep electronic communication in an acceptably polite form.

Netmeeting – This Microsoft plug in allows a moving video picture to be contained within a web page. It is now integrated into Windows Media Player.

Netscape – After Microsoft's Internet Explorer, Netscape is the most popular browser software available for surfing the internet. An excellent browser, Netscape has suffered in the wake of Internet Explorer, mainly because of the success of Microsoft in getting the latter pre-loaded on most new PCs. Netscape Communicator comes complete with email, newsgroups, address book and bookmarks, plus a web page composer, and you can adjust its settings in all sorts of useful ways. Netscape was taken over by American Online for $4 billion.

nettie – Slang term for someone who spends a lot of time on the internet.

newbie – Popular term for a new member of a newsgroup or mailing list.

newsgroup – A Usenet discussion group. Each newsgroup is a collection of messages, usually unedited and not checked by anyone ('unmoderated'). Messages can be placed within the newsgroup by anyone including you. It is rather like reading and sending public emails. The ever-growing newsgroups have been around for much longer than the world wide web, and are an endless source of information, gossip, news, entertainment, sex, politics, resources and ideas. The 50,000-plus newsgroups are collectively referred to as Usenet, and millions of people use it every day.

news reader – A type of software that enables you to search, read, post and manage messages in a newsgroup. It will normally be supplied by your internet service provider when you first sign up, or preloaded on your new computer. The best known are Microsoft Outlook, and Netscape Messenger.

news server – A remote computer (e.g. your internet service provider) that enables you to access newsgroups. If you cannot get some or any newsgroups from your existing news server, use your favourite search engine to search for 'open news servers' - there are lots of them freely available. When you have found one you like, add it to your news reader by clicking on its name. The first time you do this, it may take 10 to 20 minutes to load the names of all the newsgroups onto your computer, but after that they open up in seconds whenever you want them.

nick – Nickname, an alias you can give yourself and use when entering a chat channel, rather than using your real name.

Nominet – The official body for registering domain names in the UK (for example web sites whose name ends in .co.uk).

online – The time you spend linked via a modem to the internet. You can keep your phone bill down by reducing online time. The opposite term is offline.

open source software – A type of freely modifiable software, such as Linux. A definition and more information can be found at: www.opensource.org

OS – The operating system in a computer, for example MS DOS (Microsoft Disk Operating System), or Windows 95/98/2000.

packet – The term for any small piece of data sent or received over the internet on your behalf by your internet service provider, and containing your address and the recipient's address. One email message for example may be transmitted as several different packets of information, reassembled at the other end to recreate the message.

password – A word or series of letters and numbers that enables a user to access a file, computer or program. A passphrase is a password made by using more than one word.

PC – Personal computer.

ping – You can use a ping test to check the connection speed between your computer and another computer.

Pentium – The name of a very popular microprocessor chip in personal computers, manufactured by Intel. The first Pentium IIIs were supplied with secret and unique personal identifiers, which ordinary people surfing the net were unwittingly sending out, enabling persons unknown to construct detailed user profiles. After a storm of protest, Pentium changed the technology so that this identifier could be disabled. If you buy or use a Pentium III computer you should be aware of this risk to your privacy when online.

PGP – Pretty Good Privacy. A proprietary method of encoding a message before transmitting it over the internet. With PGP, a message is first compressed then encoded with the help of keys. Just like the valuables in a locked safe, your message is safe unless a person has access to the right keys. Many governments (as in France today) would like complete access to people's private keys. New Labour wanted access to everyone's keys in the UK, but dropped the proposed legislation after widespread protests. Unlike in many countries, there is no general right to privacy in the UK.

plug in – A type of (usually free and downloadable) software required to add some form of functionality to web page viewing. A well-known example is Macromedia Shockwave, a plug in which enables you to view animations.

PoP – Point of presence. This refers to the dial up phone numbers available from your ISP. If your ISP does not have a local point of presence (i.e. local access phone number), then don't sign up - your telephone bill will rocket because you will be charged national phone rates. All the major ISPs have local numbers covering the whole of the country.

portal site – Portal means gateway. It is a web site designed to be used as a 'home base' from which you can start your web experience each time you go online. Portals often serve as general information points and offer news, weather and other information that you can customise to your own needs. Yahoo! is a good example of a portal (http://www.yahoo.com). A portal site includes the one that loads into your browser each time you connect to the internet. It could for example be the front page of your internet service provider. Or you can set your browser to make it some other front page, for example a search engine such as Yahoo!, or even your own home page if you have one.

post, to – The common term used for sending ('posting') messages to a newsgroup. Posting messages is very like sending emails, except of course that they are public and everyone can read them. Also, newsgroup postings are archived, and can be read by anyone in the world years later. Because of this, many people feel more comfortable using an 'alias' (made-up name) when posting messages.

privacy – You have practically no personal privacy online. Almost every mouse click and key stroke you make while online is being electronically logged, analysed and possibly archived by internet organisations, government agencies, police or other surveillance services. You are also leaving a permanent trail of data on whichever computer you are using. But then, if you have nothing to hide you have nothing to fear. To explore privacy issues worldwide, visit the authoritative Electronic Frontier Foundation web site at www.eff.org, and for the UK, www.netfreedom.org.

protocol – Technical term for the method by which computers communicate. A protocol is something that has been agreed and can be used between systems. For example, for viewing web pages your computer would use hypertext transfer protocol (http). For downloading and uploading files, it would use file transfer protocol (ftp). It's not something to worry too much about in ordinary life.

proxy – An intermediate computer or server, used for reasons of security.

Quicktime – A popular free software program from Apple Computers. It is designed to play sounds and images including video clips and animations on both Apple Macs and personal computers.

radio button – A field on a feedback form which allows you to make a choice from a list of alternatives.

Glossary . . . .

refresh, reload – The refresh or reload button on your browser toolbar tells the web page you are looking at to reload.

register – You may have to give your name, personal details and financial information to some sites before you can continue to use the pages. Site owners may want to produce a mailing list to offer you products and services. Registration is also used to discourage casual traffic.

registered user – Someone who has filled out an online form and then been granted permission to access a restricted area of a web site. Access is usually obtained by logging on, typically by entering a password and user name.

remailer – A remailer preserves your privacy by acting as a go-between when you browse or send email messages. An anonymous remailer is simply a computer connected to the internet that can forward an email message to other people after stripping off the header of the messages. Once a message is routed through an anonymous remailer, the recipient of that message, or anyone intercepting it, can no longer identify its origin.

RFC – Request for comment. RFCs are the way that the internet developers propose changes and discuss standards and procedures. See http://rs.internic.net.

RSA – One of the most popular methods of encryption, and used in Netscape browsers. See http://www.rsa.com.

router – A machine that direct internet data (network packets) from one place to another.

search engine – A search engine is a web site you can use for finding something on the internet. Popular search engines are big web sites and information directories in their own right. There are hundreds of them; the best known include Alta Vista, Excite, Google, Infoseek, Lycos and Yahoo!.

secure servers – The hardware and software provided so that people can use their credit cards and leave other details without the risk of others seeing them online. Your browser will indicate when you are entering a secure site.

secure sockets layer (SSL) – A standard piece of technology which ensures secure financial transactions and data flow over the internet.

security certificate – Information that is used by the SSL protocol to establish a secure connection. Security certificates contain information about who it belongs to, who it was issued by, some form of unique identification, valid dates, and an encrypted fingerprint that can be used to verify the contents of the certificate. In order for an SSL connection to be created both sides must have a valid security certificate.

server – Any computer on a network that provides access and serves information to other computers.

shareware – Software that you can try before you buy. Usually there is some kind of limitation such as an expiry date. To get the registered version, you must pay for the software, typically $20 to $40. A vast amount of shareware is now available on the internet.

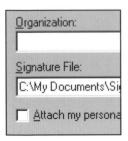

Shockwave – A popular piece of software produced by Macromedia, which enables you to view animations and other special effects on web sites. You can download it free and in a few minutes from Macromedia's web site. The effects can be fun, but they slow down the speed at which the pages load into your browser window.

signature file – This is a little text file in which you can place your address details, for adding to email and newsgroup messages. Once you have created a signature file, it is appended automatically to your emails. You can of course delete or edit it.

Slashdot – One of the leading technology news web sites, found at: http://slashdot.org

smiley – A form of **emoticon**.

snail mail – The popular term for the standard postal service involving postpersons, vans, trains, planes, sacks and sorting offices.

spam – The popular term for electronic junk mail - unsolicited and unwelcome email messages sent across the internet. The term comes from Monty Python. There are various forms of spam-busting software which you can now obtain to filter out unwanted email messages.

sniffer – A program on a computer system (usually an ISP's system) designed to collect information. Sniffers are often used by hackers to collect passwords and user names.

SSL – Secure socket layer, a key part of internet security technology.

subscribe – The term for accessing a newsgroup in order to read and post messages in the newsgroup. There is no charge, and you can subscribe, unsubscribe and resubscribe at will with a click of your mouse. Unless you post a message, no-one in the newsgroup will know that you have subscribed or unsubscribed.

surfing – Slang term for browsing the internet, especially following trails of links on pages across the world wide web.

sysop – Systems operator, someone rather like a moderator for example of a chat room or bulletin board service.

target – An area in a web page/web site which has control transferred to it from a hyperlink (see **anchor**).

TCP/IP – Transmission control protocol/internet protocol, the essential technology of the internet. It's not normally something you need worry about.

telnet – Software that allows you to connect via the internet to a remote computer and work as if you were a terminal linked to that system.

theme – A term in web page design. A theme describes the general colours and graphics used within a web site. Many themes are available in the form of readymade templates.

thumbnail – A small version of a graphic file which, when clicked, expands to full size.

thread – An ongoing topic in a Usenet newsgroup or mailing list discussion. The term refers to the original message on a particular topic, and all the replies and other messages which spin off from it. With news reading software, you can easily 'view thread' and thus read the related messages in a convenient batch.

traceroute – A program that traces the route from your machine to a remote system. It is useful if you need to discover a person's ISP, for example in the case of a spammer.

traffic – The amount of data flowing across the internet to a particular web site, newsgroup or chat room, or as emails.

trojan horse – A program that seems to perform a useful task but is really a malevolent program designed to cause damage to a computer system.

uploading – The act of copying files from your PC to a server or other PC on the internet, for example when you are publishing your own web pages. The term is most commonly used to describe the act of copying HTML pages onto the internet via FTP.

UNIX – This is a computer operating system that has been in use for many years, and still is used in many larger systems. Most ISPs use it.

Glossary ....

URL – Uniform resource locator the address of each internet page. For instance the URL of Internet Handbooks is http://www.internet-handbooks.co.uk

Usenet – The collection of well over 50,000 active newsgroups that make up a substantial part of the internet.

virtual reality – The presentation of a lifelike scenario in electronic form. It can be used for gaming, business or educational purposes.

virus – A computer program maliciously designed to cause havoc to people's computer files. Viruses can typically be received when downloading program files from the internet, or from copying material from infected disks. Even Word files can now be infected. You can protect yourself from the vast majority of them by installing some inexpensive anti-virus software, such as Norton, McAfee or Dr Solomon.

web authoring – Creating HTML pages to upload onto the internet. You will be a web author if you create your own home page for uploading onto the internet.

web client – Another term for a browser.

Webcrawler – A popular internet search engine used to find pages relating to specific keywords entered.

webmaster – Any person who manages a web site.

web page – Any single page of information you can view on the world wide web. A typical web page includes a unique URL (address), headings, text, images, and hyperlinks (usually in the form of graphic icons, or underlined text). One web page usually contains links to lots of other web pages, either within the same web site or elsewhere on the world wide web.

web rings – A network of interlinked web sites that share a common interest.

Whois – A network service that allows you to consult a database containing information about someone. A whois query can, for example, help to find the identity of someone who is sending you unwanted email messages.

Windows – The ubiquitous operating system for personal computers developed by Bill Gates and the Microsoft Corporation. The Windows 3.1 version was followed by Windows 95, further enhanced by Windows 98. Windows 2000 is the latest.

WWW – The world wide web. Since it began in 1994 this has become the most popular part of the internet. The web is now made up of more than a billion web pages of every imaginable description, typically linking to other pages. Developed by the British computer scientist, Tim Berners-Lee, its growth has been exponential and is set to continue so.

WYSIWYG – 'What you see is what you get.' If you see it on the screen, then it should look just the same when you print it out.

Yahoo! – Probably the world's most popular internet directory and search engine, and now valued on Wall Street at billions of dollars: http://www.yahoo.com

zip/unzip – Many files that you download from the internet will be in compressed format, especially if they are large files. This is to make them quicker to download. These files are said to be zipped or compressed. Unzipping these compressed files means returning them to their original size on receipt. Zip files have the extension '.zip' and are created (and unzipped) using WinZip or a similar popular software package.

Visit the free Internet HelpZone at
www.internet-handbooks.co.uk
Helping you master the internet

Useful sources

Some web design resources on the web

Clipart	http://www.clipart.com
FreeFind	http://www.freefind.com
HTML Goodies	http://www.htmlgoodies.com
HTML Guru	http://members.aol.com/htmlguru/
HTML Tutorials	http://www.dtp-aus.com
HTML Writers Guild	http://www.hwg.org
Site Gadgets	http://www.sitegadgets.com
Sizzling Jalfrezi	http://vzone.virgin.net/sizzlingjalfrezi/
Web Builder	http://www.netmag.co.uk
Web Site Garage	http://www.websitegarage.com
Webmonkey	http://hotwired.lycos.com/webmonkey/

Some web sites to visit

BBC	http://www.bbc.co.uk
Carry On Films	http://www.carryonline.com
Central Intelligence Agency (CIA)	http://www.cia.gov
Computer Word Search	http://www.webopedia.com
Computer Word Search	http://www.whatis.com
Country Walks	http://www.countrywalks.org.uk
Economist	http://www.economist.co.uk
Encyclopedia Britannica	http://www.britannica.com
Federal Bureau of Investigation (FBI)	http://www.fbi.gov
ITN News	http://www.itn.co.uk
Meteorological Office	http://www.meto.gov.uk
NASA	http://www.nasa.gov
NetDoctor	http://www.netdoctor.co.uk
NHS Direct	http://www.nhsdirect.nhs.uk
Ten Downing Street	http://www.number-10.gov.uk
Vatican	http://www.vatican.va

Some web design company sites

Active Graphics	http://www.activegraphics.co.uk	Aberdeen
ADM Design	http://www.adm-design.co.uk	Huddersfield
Alphawaves	http://www.alphawaves.net	Dumfries
Artery Design	http://www.arterydesign.co.uk	Guildford
Baracus Web Design	http://www.baracus.com	
Bluecheese	http://www.bluecheese.co.uk	Bath
Center Designs	http://www.centerdesigns.co.uk	Birmingham
Compuworks	http://Qqq.compuworks.co.uk	London
Creative Media	http://www.cmedia.co.uk	West Glamorgan
Datanet	http://www.data.net.uk	Hampshire

Useful sources...

Dream Studio	http://www.dreamstudio.co.uk	London
FB Enterprises	http://www.fisher-brothers.co.uk	Cumbria
Free Form Graphics	http://www.freeform.co.uk	Norwich
Fresh Milk Web Design	http://www.fresh-milk.co.uk	Stockport
Hyperion Media	http://www.hyperion-media.co.uk	Dorset
Lites Ltd	http://www.litesltd.co.uk	Swindon
Luminous Works	http://www.luminousworks.com	Staines
N21 Internet	http://www.n21internet.co.uk	Liverpool
NetStyles	http://www.netstyles.co.uk	Rochdale
Red Rhino Interactive	http://www.rerhino.co.uk	Armagh, NI
Saturn Designs	http://www.saturndesigns.co.uk	Milton Keynes
SBD Partnership	http://www.indesign.net	Whitley Bay
Sodaweb	http://www.sodaweb.co.uk	Berkshire
VillaSanta	http://www.villasanta.co.uk	Northamptonshire
Webspinners	http://www.webspinners.co.uk	

Index

Index...